THE ROYAL BRITISH LEGION

YEARS OF HEROES

MATT CROUCHER GC

OFFICIAL 90TH ANNIVERSARY TRIBUTE

Collins

First published in 2011 by Collins

HarperCollins*Publishers*
77–85 Fulham Palace Road
London W6 8JB

www.harpercollins.co.uk

13 12 11 10 09
9 8 7 6 5 4 3 2 1

Text © Matt Croucher 2011

The author asserts his moral right to be identified as the author of this work.

A catalogue record for this book is available from the British Library.

ISBN: 978-0-00-744153-2

Publishing Director: Iain MacGregor
Project Editor: Kathy Dyke
Editor: Patricia Briggs
Picture Research: Marcus Cowper and Elen Jones
Production: Anna Mitchelmore

Designed by Joanna MacGregor

Printed and bound in Great Britain by Butler Tanner and Dennis Ltd

Find out more about HarperCollins and the environment at
www.harpercollins.co.uk/green

FOREWORD

It is a great privilege to introduce the Royal British Legion's *90 Years of Heroes*. I have had the honour of commanding British Forces at every level from platoon upwards over the past 40 years and have learned many things about heroism. While it is clear that those represented in this book represent the very best of our people and our nation, there are heroes among our men and women other than those who wear medals.

Every time I go to visit troops in Helmand or at an air station or on a warship, I am reminded of the raw courage needed by so many to do their daily jobs, willingly going on patrols that they know put them in harm's way, consciously diving in dangerous waters or flying over enemy positions which test their nerves, as any moment could change their future for ever. This quiet courage, the kind that is often unreported and too often unrewarded, is the ordinary, daily life for many of the young men and women I am so honoured to lead. It reminds me of the times my father did much the same in the Second World War and others, including my grandfather, did the same nearly a century ago.

The title *90 Years of Heroes* applies just as well to the Royal British Legion. Over the years the Legion has heroically defended the rights of servicemen and servicewomen who have returned from combat to find the hardest challenges before them – adapting to life-changing injuries and getting on with ordinary life. This quiet heroism, and the heroism of those who supported and still support them, is a vital part of what makes the Legion so essential to the fabric of our military covenant.

For all these reasons I am honoured to be part of this appeal for the Royal British Legion and look forward to the book exceeding all fundraising targets.

General Sir David Richards
GCB, CBE, DSO, ADC Gen.

INTRODUCTION

▲ Outside Buckingham
Palace after receiving
my medal from the
Queen.

Ever since I can remember, I have been aware of the Royal British Legion and what it stands for, from my mum pinning a poppy to my chest and taking me along to church on Remembrance Sunday when I was a toddler, right through to the present day, when I have more direct involvement in fundraising and am a representative for the charity.

Even though my immediate family weren't in the military, my wider family have always served in the forces. My uncle was a British Army officer, my grandfather was an active Royal Naval officer during the Second World War, and the links continue back through our family tree.

I have always had a passionate interest in the military and planned to join at the earliest possible opportunity. And so I became an Air Training Corps cadet at 13. Although I enjoyed the RAF side of the military, and the flying in particular appealed to me, my passion lay with getting all camouflaged up and running round the woods.

From the age of 14 my ambition was to join the Royal Marines. They had the longest and hardest basic training of any elite force in NATO and I had bought a video all about it. I was keen on sports when I was young, particularly athletics, football, martial arts, boxing and rugby and this, allied with my enjoyment of running around at cadets with a rifle and wearing camouflage, made me think the Royal Marines would be ideal for me.

In the year 2000 I passed my aptitude, medical and selection tests for the Royal Marines and soon began training. Without question, it was the hardest and most challenging thing I've ever done. It was daunting at the age of 16, starting training with 60 other recruits, knowing that about two-thirds of you weren't going to make it and there were huge obstacles to overcome. Each day over the next nine months brought new challenges and pushed me that little bit harder. It was totally worth it at the end, though – when I received my coveted green beret it was one of the proudest moments of my life.

Since then I have undertaken two tours of duty in Iraq with the Royal Marines, one working for the United Nations. More recently I have undertaken a tour in Afghanistan, and was subsequently awarded the George Cross by Her Majesty

Queen Elizabeth II at Buckingham Palace on 30 October 2008. Nothing can prepare you for receiving a Class I medal and I'm sure everyone else who has received either a George Cross or Victoria Cross will tell you the same: it brings overwhelming media attention, followed by an abundance of requests!

It took a good 12–18 months for me to feel grounded again and to get used to these new pressures and responsibilities. I was offered all kinds of TV shows and appearances but I didn't really feel comfortable with any of that.

I decided to turn my attention to raising awareness and money for military charities. To tell the truth, this was made a lot easier by the fact I had a George Cross. Doors opened that would normally remain closed, and people who would ordinarily ignore you were overjoyed to assist. I've obtained items for auctions that have raised five-figure sums, raised thousands through book signings and worked with many individuals to help their events raise as much as possible. I'm glad to say that to date I've helped raise well over £100,000 for Forces' charities as well as giving my advice, guidance and support to a number of others. I'm continuing the tradition with this book for the Royal British Legion's 90th Anniversary, which I hope will raise another £100,000 before Christmas 2011.

I don't consider myself any more of a hero than anyone else who serves Queen and Country. Other Marines would have done exactly the same as I did if I hadn't been fulfilling that role that night. I've witnessed some very brave feats by individuals, and many have gone unrecognised.

The people I've featured in this book have done more than the 'odd thing' for their country or the Royal British Legion. They're people that stick out from the crowd; people who have contributed hugely to our society and worked tirelessly to protect what we call Great Britain and make it the free country we enjoy today. Life would be very different if it weren't for people like these, making great sacrifices in order to uphold what we believe in. And this is why I feel so passionately about our servicemen and women and the aftercare and support they should receive. It is my aim over this 90th Anniversary year to raise as much money as possible for the Royal British Legion, because our veterans deserve it.

During these times of financial cuts, restraints and hardship, please spare a thought for our military personnel active all over the world, often working for wages far lower than the national average and conditions far worse than those common in Great Britain:

- Mechanic Gary, who has a patch of desert, a tent and an endless queue of vehicles to fix for the next six months, working extra long hours, seven days a week in 50°C heat.
- Marine Steve, who has spent the last two months getting shot at every day and who has just witnessed his best friend being blown up.
- Pilot Michelle, who works around the clock, maximising her flying hours each day to deliver troops, food, ammo and medical supplies around the battle zone, always at the risk of being shot down.
- Navy medic Sam, whose skills have never been put to the test before: suddenly he has to treat four critically wounded casualties whilst under fire, prioritising who has the best chance of survival and working on them first. The nearest hospital is 100 miles away and the nearest evacuation helicopter is 20 minutes away.

The ninety people you are about to discover, spanning the period the Royal British Legion has been in existence, demonstrate the wide variety of military and peacetime experiences our country has lived through. From the inter-war years, through the global conflict with Nazi Germany and its Fascist allies, to the many 'police actions', our servicemen and women have displayed their unique courage in winning whatever personal action they found themselves in. Naturally we will also read about modern-day heroes, seeing action in the Falklands, as well as in Bosnia, Iraq and Afghanistan.

I have tried to find a hero for every year; and whether it is because they actually saw service in that period, or happened to have been born, or in some cases, died that year, this takes the reader on a thorough journey through British military life over the past nine decades. I hope you enjoy discovering these men and women's deeds and exploits just as much as I did when researching the book with my co-writer, Marcus Cowper.

Matt Croucher GC

CHAPTER ONE

Foundation and early steps

The First World War had inflicted death on a grand scale on those who participated in it, the unparalleled level of mobilisation led to matching numbers of casualties, and the government of the day was overwhelmed by the task of trying to provide for those who had been afflicted. There was a clear need for an organisation to represent the voices of those left widowed or disabled by the war to end all wars.

Even before the end of the First World War, efforts were underway to provide a voice for those who had served in the British armed forces. In fact, three completely separate organisations had formed by the end of 1917: the National Association of Discharged Sailors and Soldiers, founded in Blackburn in 1916 and loosely affiliated with the Trades Union movement and the Labour Party; the National Federation of Discharged and Demobilised Sailors and Soldiers, based in London and with links to the Liberal Party; and the Comrades of the Great War, a non-political organisation that nonetheless had extensive links with the establishment of the day. These three organisations were joined by

the left-wing National Union of Ex-servicemen following the end of the First World War in November 1918. A number of efforts were made to unite these disparate groups, but it was not until the foundation of the United Services Fund, containing some £7 million in canteen profits from the war, that they managed to combine in order to ensure the fair distribution of the fund throughout the country.

At the same time, Field Marshal the Earl Haig, the commander of the British Expeditionary Force during the First World War, had been leading a fundraising campaign for a united organisation providing assistance to ex-officers, the Officers Association. It became clear that a single body representing all these interests would best serve the needs of those whom they sought to help.

In 1920 a conference brought about the amalgamation of all these bodies, ratified by their individual members. On 14 May 1921 the new unified organisation was founded under the name the British Legion, with the Prince of Wales as its patron and Earl Haig as its first president.

The Legion had much to do. The first Poppy Appeal was launched the same year, widely

▼ *With so many servicemen returning to civilian life, unemployment was rife. One of the newly formed Legion's roles was to help find work for these men.*

1921 — Foundation of the British Legion; the first Poppy Appeal

1922

1923

1924 — Establishment of Remembrance Sunday following a Legion suggestion

1925 — Legion takes over Preston Hall, later the site of the Legion Village

◀ The Legion was also heavily involved in the commemoration of the First World War, and organised a pilgrimage of some 11,000 people to the battlefields of the Western Front in 1928.

▼ An early Legion poster promoting the Poppy Appeal that did so much so fund the Legion's activities.

supported by Earl Haig and timed to coincide with Armistice Day, 11 November. This proved to be an enormous success and provided the funds for the Legion to support those affected by the First World War, either directly – in terms of financial aid, employment or housing – or by raising political awareness of their plight through constant campaigning. The Legion was also central to the commemoration of the conflict, being deeply involved in the establishment of 11 November as Remembrance Day, and the later adoption of Remembrance Sunday, while 1927 saw the first Legion-organised Festival of Remembrance.

With the passing of Earl Haig in 1928, the Legion played a central role in his funeral. This was a moment of national mourning, for Haig's reputation was as yet untouched by criticism of his wartime tactics and planning, and the Legion's role underlined how quickly it had become a significant part of British national life.

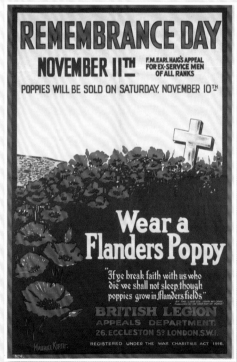

REMEMBRANCE DAY
NOVEMBER 11TH
F.M. EARL HAIG'S APPEAL
FOR EX-SERVICE MEN
OF ALL RANKS
POPPIES WILL BE SOLD ON SATURDAY. NOVEMBER 10TH

Wear a
Flanders Poppy

"If ye break faith with us who die we shall not sleep though poppies grow in Flanders fields."

BRITISH LEGION
APPEALS DEPARTMENT.
26. ECCLESTON S? LONDON. S.W.I.
REGISTERED UNDER THE WAR CHARITIES ACT 1916.

1926	1927	1928	1929	1930
	First Festival of Remembrance at the Albert Hall	Death of Earl Haig, the first President of the Legion to organise celebrations		

CAPTAIN ISHAR SINGH
VC, OBI

awarded 25 November 1921 • Waziristan • 28th Punjabis

▼ *A marching column on the Northwest Frontier in the early 1930s, consisting of British infantry and pack-mule transport.*

Ishar Singh was the first Sikh to be awarded the Victoria Cross for his bravery when the convoy he was protecting was attacked by tribesmen in Waziristan in April 1921.

Waziristan had been the scene of a revolt against British rule from 1919 to 1920. The rugged frontier territory was a perfect location for ambushes, and the region has been a source of conflict for the British, Indian and now Pakistani Armies from the First Anglo-Afghan War through to the present day.

While British and Indian forces had been preoccupied by the First World War, the Waziris had launched a series of raids against British positions and supply columns, and this intensified in the wake of the Third Anglo-Afghan War of 1919 into a large-scale revolt. Although this rebellion had been largely put down by the end of 1920, there were still a number of raids throughout 1921 and it was in one of these that Sepoy Ishar Singh was awarded his VC.

Entering the Indian Army in 1913, Ishar Singh had served throughout the First World War in Ceylon, Mesopotamia, Palestine and Egypt, before his regiment was posted to Waziristan in 1919 to help put down the revolt.

On 10 April 1921 he was part of the escort for a camel convoy when rebellious tribesmen ambushed the column in a narrow gorge. Ishar Singh was the Number 1 of a Lewis gun section and in the immediate aftermath of the attack he was seriously wounded in the chest and lost hold of his Lewis gun. The initial assault had killed all the officers of his company and, realising the seriousness of the situation, he immediately counter-attacked, along with two colleagues, and succeeded in wresting back his weapon, which he then manned until reinforcements arrived. Despite being ordered to report for medical attention, Ishar Singh helped the medical officer for the next three hours, bringing water for the wounded and protecting the injured and the officer from enemy fire, until he became too weak from loss of blood and finally received medical attention.

Following the award of his medal, Ishar Singh travelled to London in 1929 to attend a dinner for VC recipients. He was later one of Edward VIII's Indian orderly officers in 1936. He died on 2 December 1963.

◀ *Ishar Singh VC, the first Sikh to be awarded the VC.*

The Lewis gun was the standard light machine gun used by the British and Indian Armies throughout the First World War and during the interwar years. Although formally replaced in 1938, it continued to see limited service in the Second World War. The brainchild of US Army officer Colonel Isaac Newton Lewis, its portability, high rate of fire and versatility made it one of the outstanding machine guns of the First World War.

DAVID LLOYD GEORGE, FIRST EARL LLOYD GEORGE OF DWYFOR OM

▼ David Lloyd George carrying the pole of 'patriotism' while balancing on the political tightrope. This wooden caricature figure was made at the Lord Roberts Memorial Workshops for Disabled Soldiers and Sailors in Fulham, London, during the First World War, and was subsequently sold for charity.

David Lloyd George was a social reformer and British Prime Minister who led Britain to victory over Germany and her allies, despite ruling over a coalition government and having very difficult relations with military leaders.

In December 1916, while Britain was in the throes of the First World War, Prime Minister Herbert Asquith was forced out of office and his place was taken by David Lloyd George, the son of a Welsh schoolmaster. The war was not going well and Lloyd George had a seemingly impossible job ahead of him.

One of the first things that he did was to create a small, five-man War Cabinet responsible for making the essential decisions about the running of the war. This new Cabinet was intended to end the drawn-out discussions of the previous cabinet, which had often resulted in indecision, hampering the war effort. The War Cabinet was considered to be a great success. It met every day during the war and was responsible for all major military, diplomatic and economic decisions. An Imperial War Cabinet was also created, which included representatives from around the Empire.

Lloyd George was not on the best of terms with military leaders and he constantly tried to reduce their power. However, the endless clashes between government and military simply resulted in more difficulties when trying to plan a successful wartime strategy. One of his most tragic failures was his inability to stop the Passchendaele offensive in the summer of 1917. Despite arguing against it, he was outvoted and it went ahead, resulting in the loss of as many as a quarter of a million British soldiers by its end in November of that year. However, he did succeed in creating the Supreme War Council at Versailles, which was used to coordinate allied military strategy. His main aim had been to reduce the authority of William Robertson, the Chief of the Imperial General Staff, and Douglas Haig, the Commander-in-Chief of the army.

In this, he was to some extent successful, as Robertson resigned.

Lloyd George did have one resounding military success during the course of the war. As the loss of shipping to U-boat attacks grew, he insisted on the adoption of a convoy system by the navy. By the end of 1917, the system had been implemented and was considered a success, with losses being significantly reduced.

Lloyd George went on to lead Britain to eventual victory in November 1918 and was hailed as a great wartime leader. After the war, he was re-elected and played a significant role in the negotiation of the Treaty of Versailles.

At home, he continued with his attempts at social reform, determined to rebuild a nation fit for heroes. However, he was part of a coalition government and many members did not back his plan. By 1922 he had lost a lot of support and found himself embroiled in a major scandal over the sale of honours. He resigned as Prime Minister in October 1922, although he remained active in politics into the 1940s. He died of cancer on 26 March 1945.

▶ *David Lloyd George in 1919, following the end of the First World War.*

▼ *Crowds waving and smiling around the Victoria Memorial outside Buckingham Palace in London on Armistice Day.*

LIEUTENANT ARTHUR WESLEY WHEEN

MM AND TWO BARS

awarded 21 September 1916 • Western Front • AIF

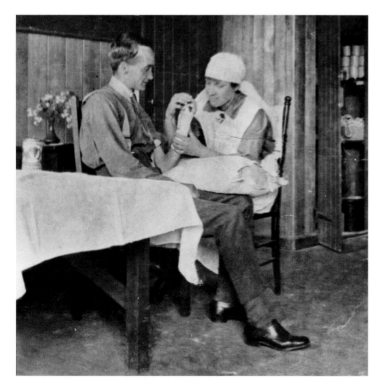

▼ *Lieutenant Arthur Wesley Wheen of the 54th Battalion, AIF, having his hand dressed at a military hospital.*

Arthur Wesley Wheen, a renowned academic most famous for coining the phrase 'All Quiet on the Western Front', was an unlikely hero whose bravery during the First World War earned him the Military Medal with two Bars.

Arthur Wheen graduated from Oxford University in 1923 and began his career as a librarian and translator. However, by the time he graduated from Oxford, he had fought not only on the Western Front but also in Egypt, showing bravery and dedication when confronted with the horrors of the battlefields of the First World War.

Australian by birth, Arthur Wheen joined the Australian Imperial Force (AIF) in 1915 and spent the first few months of 1916 as a signaller in Tel-el-Kebir in Egypt. In June 1916 he was posted to France and it was here that he showed the strength of character for which he would be remembered in later life. At Petillon in July 1916, while under heavy artillery fire, he repaired telephone wires that had been cut and managed to maintain communications 'at great personal risk and self-sacrifice', a feat for which he was awarded the MM in September 1916. He went on to be awarded the first Bar for action at Beaulencourt in March 1917 and the second Bar for action at Villers-Bretonneux in April

ALL QUIET ON THE WESTERN FRONT

1918. He was wounded twice in action, the first time in September 1917 and again in September 1918, and was eventually sent home as an invalid, arriving in Sydney in March 1919.

Having been chosen as a Rhodes Scholar, Wheen read Modern History at New College, Oxford, graduating with third-class honours owing to health problems. After graduation, he accepted the job of assistant librarian at the Victoria and Albert Museum in London. It was here that he was instrumental in shaping the library, which is now known as the National Art Library.

Wheen was a brilliant linguist, and is most famous for his work as a translator. In 1929 he translated Erich Maria Remarque's *Im Westen nichts Neues*, the title of which he translated as *All Quiet on the Western Front*, a phrase that is still used in common parlance to this day. He translated a number of other works, including two more novels by Remarque, and also wrote one short story, called 'Two Maters'. He went on to become Keeper of the library in 1945, a post he held until his retirement in 1962.

Arthur Wheen passed away on 15 March 1971 in Amersham Hospital. This brave soldier and noble scholar is best summed up by his obituary in *The Times*, where he is described as 'a man of great sweetness of nature, kindness and generosity of heart'.

◀ *A poster dating from 1930 advertising the film* All Quiet on the Western Front, *directed by Lewis Milestone.*

▼ *A machine-gun position established by the 54th Battalion, AIF, during the morning of the attack through Peronne on 2 September 1918.*

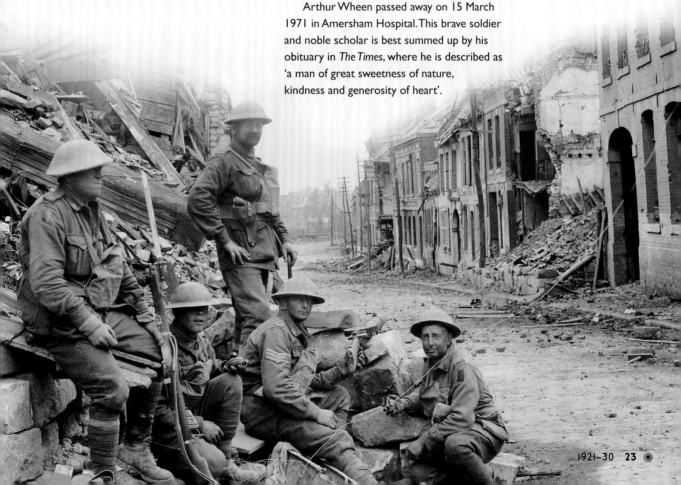

CAPTAIN FREDERICK JOHN 'JOHNNIE' WALKER

CB, DSO AND THREE BARS

awarded (DSO) 6 January 1942 • Battle of the Atlantic • Royal Navy

▼ Captain 'Johnnie' Walker on the search for U-boats in the Western Approaches.

Captain 'Johnnie' Walker was the most successful anti-submarine warfare commander of the Second World War, sinking more U-boats during the Battle of the Atlantic than any other Allied commander.

Frederick Walker's journey to achieving this accolade might have been said to have started in 1924, with the establishment of the anti-submarine training school at Portland (HMS *Osprey*). Walker took a training course there in 1926 and went on to become a specialist in the field, using his expertise in a number of postings during the interwar years.

However, by the start of the Second World War, it seemed as though Walker's career was over. Having been passed over for promotion to captain, he had been due to take early retirement, a plan put on hold by the commencement of war. In 1940 he became Staff Officer (Operations) to Vice-Admiral Sir Bertram Ramsay. Although this was an important anti-submarine role, Walker still wanted to have command of his own ship so that he could try out the tactics he had formulated. This ambition was fulfilled in October 1941, when he was given command of the 36th Escort Group and HMS *Stork*. He was now able to put into practice his belief that a combined attack from both air and sea would effectively combat the U-boat threat while keeping the convoy protected.

His first contact with U-boats happened when his group was escorting home the 32 ships of the HG76 convoy from Gibraltar in December 1941. Five U-boats were sunk during the journey and Walker was awarded the Distinguished Service Order 'for daring, skill and determination while escorting to this country a valuable Convoy in the face of relentless attacks from the Enemy'. Walker's group destroyed at

least three more U-boats before he became Captain (D) Liverpool in September 1942. He was awarded a Bar to his DSO in July 1942.

His next command was 2 Support Group and HMS *Starling*, which he took charge of in February 1943. He continued to successfully combat the U-boats using his innovative techniques, and in September 1943 he was appointed a Companion of the Bath for 'leadership and daring in command of HMS *Starling* in successful actions against Enemy submarines in the Atlantic'. He was awarded a second Bar to his DSO in February 1944.

Walker's final task was to protect the fleet during the D-Day invasions in June 1944. For two weeks he worked without respite. He and his group were relentless and no U-boat managed to get past them. For his valiant efforts he was awarded the third Bar to his DSO on 13 June 1944.

Captain Frederick Walker's dedication to duty finally took its tragic toll. On 7 July 1944 he suffered a cerebral thrombosis, thought to have been caused by exhaustion, and on 9 July 1944 he died, at the age of 48. It is thought that over 1000 people attended his funeral service at Liverpool Anglican Cathedral to pay tribute him. He was buried at sea.

▼ HMS Stork was a Bittern-class sloop famous for being the first operational command of the then Commander 'Johnnie' Walker.

LIEUTENANT COLONEL THOMAS EDWARD LAWRENCE

CB, DSO

awarded (DSO) 10 May 1918 • Tafilah • British Army

▶ *T. E. Lawrence as Aircraftman T. E. Shaw on the aerodrome at Miranshah Fort in Waziristan, India.*

▼ *Lieutenant Colonel T. E. Lawrence, CB, DSO, by James McBey 1918.*

T. E. Lawrence is arguably the most famous soldier of his generation. Dubbed 'Lawrence of Arabia' for his role during the Arab Revolt, he was known not only for his wartime exploits but also for his writing.

Tired of the repressive regime of the Ottoman Turks, the Arabs rose up and revolted in 1916, with the aim of creating a free Arab state. The Ottoman Empire was one of the Central Powers fighting against the Allies in the First World War and so the British and the French allied themselves with the Arabs in June 1916. A number of British officials were then sent out to assist with the revolt, one of whom was a young army captain named Thomas Edward Lawrence.

Lawrence's role in the conflict has become legend and he has been immortalised on page and screen. However, it often comes as a surprise that he was involved in only one conventional battle – the Battle of Tafilah, which took place in January 1918. Tafilah, a hill town to the south-east of the Dead Sea, was of strategic importance to the Arabs and the only way to hold on to the town was to fight a pitched battle against the Turks. On the morning of 26 January, the Arabs were in place

> *... conspicuous gallantry and devotion to duty in an engagement. He showed splendid leadership and skill, and was largely responsible for the success of the action in which 300 prisoners, two field guns, and twenty-three machine guns were captured.*

in defensive positions when the Turks attacked. They were assailed with a deluge of shells and machine-gun fire, and at one point it seemed as though they would be overrun. However, in true Hollywood style, reinforcements appeared just in time and the Turks were struck from behind on both sides. They suffered horrific casualties, with at least 200 being killed and more than 250 captured. The Arab casualties were 25 dead and 40 wounded. A blizzard started later in the day and although the Arab wounded were carried to safety, the Turkish wounded were left on the battlefield to die overnight. This action is justified by Lawrence, who states in *The Seven Pillars of Wisdom*: 'We risked our lives in the blizzard… to save our own fellows; and if our rule was not to lose Arabs to kill even many Turks, still less might we lose them to save Turks.'

For his role in the battle Lawrence was awarded the Distinguished Service Order for: 'conspicuous gallantry and devotion to duty in an engagement. He showed splendid leadership and skill, and was largely responsible for the success of the action in which 300 prisoners, two field guns, and twenty-three machine guns were captured.'

However, he felt no joy in victory, stating that 'there was no glory left but the terror of the broken flesh, which had been our own men, carried past us to their homes.'

After the war Lawrence joined the Foreign Office and then the RAF. He left the RAF in February 1935, and a couple of months later, tragically, he died of injuries sustained in a motorcycle accident.

SMLE, Mk 3, carried by T. E. Lawrence during the Arab revolt.

AIR MARSHAL SIR ARTHUR 'MARY' CONINGHAM

KCB, KBE, DSO, MC, DFC, AFC

awarded (MC) 17 September 1917 • RAF

▶ *Air Vice Marshal A. Coningham, DSO, MC, DFC, AFC, by Eric Kennington.*

▼ *Air Vice Marshal Sir Arthur Coningham, Commander of the Western Desert Air Force, standing outside his mobile headquarters, a caravan in the Western Desert.*

Sir Arthur 'Mary' Coningham is best remembered as a brilliant strategist whose air-land tactics revolutionised the battlefields of North Africa in the Second World War. However, he was also an exceptional pilot and ace who achieved 14 aerial victories in the final two years of the First World War.

Arthur Coningham was born in Australia and brought up in New Zealand. His early military career was spent firstly with the 5th Wellington Regiment and then with the Canterbury Mounted Rifles. In 1915, he was taken ill, and he was discharged from the Army in spring 1916 as unfit for further service. Almost immediately he sailed for England and joined the Royal Flying Corps, then was trained as a pilot, commissioned and sent to France in December 1916. In France he joined No. 32 Squadron, flying the DH2.

It was on the Western Front that he came into his own. In the seven months that he flew with No. 32 Squadron he is credited with ten kills. Nine of his victories occurred in the month of July while flying the DH5, and three of these happened on the same day, 20 July. For his actions during this time he was awarded the

> " ... conspicuous gallantry and devotion to duty in attacking enemy aircraft. On numerous occasions he has displayed great dash and a fine offensive spirit in engaging the enemy at close range, and driving them down completely out of control. "

Distinguished Service Order for: 'conspicuous gallantry and devotion to duty. With three other pilots he attacked an enemy machine which was protected by ten others, shot it down, and destroyed another one the same evening. Shortly afterwards he and two others attacked five of the enemy, and although wounded and rendered unconscious for the moment, he succeeded in driving down two of the enemy. In spite of being much exhausted by loss of blood he continued his patrol until he was sure that no more enemy machines were in the vicinity, setting a splendid example of pluck and determination.' And he was awarded the Military Cross for: 'conspicuous gallantry and devotion to duty in attacking enemy aircraft. On numerous occasions he has displayed great dash and a fine offensive spirit in engaging the enemy at close range, and driving them down completely out of control.'

Coningham was wounded at the end of July and invalided back to England. He did not return to the Western Front until July 1918 when he took command of No. 92 Squadron, then flying the SE5a. It was a very successful time for the squadron. Coningham himself scored a further four victories and was awarded the Distinguished Flying Cross on 3 June 1919 for his actions.

After the war, Coningham accepted a permanent commission in the RAF and had a number of postings, including time in the Middle East and Africa. During the Second World War he was put in command of the Western Desert Air Force and later took command of 2nd Tactical Air Force. He retired from the RAF in August 1947.

Arthur Coningham was lost, presumed dead, when the aircraft that was taking him from the Azores to Bermuda disappeared on 30 January 1948.

▼ *A Martin Baltimore of No. 69 Squadron RAF based in the Mediterranean. The light bombers of the Desert Air Force provided highly useful close air support in the course of 8th Army's victories.*

King George V following the gun carriage bearing the Unknown Warrior as it moves along Whitehall past the newly built Cenotaph on 11 November 1920. The body of the Unknown Warrior was taken to Westminster Abbey, where it was buried at the west end of the nave. Some 1 250 000 people visited the grave in the week after the funeral.

ADMIRAL OF THE FLEET DAVID BEATTY, FIRST EARL BEATTY

GCB, OM, GCVO, DSO

awarded (DSO) 17 November 1896 • Sudan • Royal Navy

▼ *A patriotic caricature model of Admiral Sir David Beatty, made by the ship's carpenters of HMS* Queen Elizabeth *around 1917 or 1918.*

Lord Beatty was the youngest British Admiral since Nelson. After an unremarkable early career, he started on the path to greatness in Sudan and China and went on to become Commander-in-Chief of the Grand Fleet and receive the surrender of the German High Seas Fleet at the end of the First World War. He retired in 1927.

Born on 17 January 1871, David Beatty joined the Navy at the age of 13. He had an undistinguished career until 1896, when he joined Kitchener's Sudan expedition as commander of one of the gunboats supporting the troops. When Colville, the commander of the river flotilla, was wounded by shore fire, Beatty took over command. He led his boats on the dangerous journey up the Nile through enemy territory to Dongola, which was successfully taken. His courage under fire and his leadership led to the award of the Distinguished Service Order in November 1896.

He rejoined Kitchener in the Sudan in June 1897, at the request of Kitchener himself. He was again commended for his service during the campaign and was promoted to commander in November 1898, at the young age of 27.

Beatty's next posting was as Executive Officer of HMS *Barfleur* of the China Station. His first year was without notable incident. However, that situation changed in the summer of 1900, when the Boxer Rebellion reached Peking and threatened foreign nationals there. Beatty was part of a land force defending Tientsin from the 15,000 Chinese troops who surrounded it, and he played a significant part in the fighting around the city. However, he was seriously wounded in the left arm and sent back to England. His bravery during the campaign had been noted and he was promoted to captain in November 1900, just two years after his

▶ *Admiral Sir David Beatty poses for journalists on board a ship.*

promotion to commander. He was 13 years younger than the average officer making the same career move. In those few years at the turn of the century, Beatty had managed to go from run-of-the-mill officer to rising star with a magnificent career ahead of him.

Although Beatty spent almost two years recovering from his wounds after the action in China, he was back in command of his own vessel in June 1902. From then he progressed rapidly up the promotions ladder and at the start of the First World War was acting vice-admiral. He played a prominent part in the war and commanded the Grand Fleet from November 1916 until the war's end.

In 1927 David Beatty, by now the First Earl Beatty, retired from service. By 1935, he was suffering from breathing difficulties brought on by a string of riding accidents and from heart strain. However, he was always a man to put duty before personal concerns and, despite his ill health, he insisted on being a pallbearer at Admiral Jellicoe's funeral in November 1935 and attending that of George V in January 1936. These actions are thought to have contributed to his death from heart failure in March 1936. He is interred in St Paul's Cathedral.

FIELD MARSHAL DOUGLAS HAIG, FIRST EARL HAIG

KT, GCB, OM, GCVO, KCIE, ADC

awarded (OM) 1919 • Western Front • British Army

Douglas Haig was one of the most controversial figures of the First World War. However, after the war he devoted his life to the welfare of ex-soldiers and their families, doing more for them than perhaps any other general in history. He died in 1928.

▼ The service dress cap worn by Haig during his time as Commander-in-Chief of the British Expeditionary Force.

On 3 February 1928, just five days after the sudden death of Field Marshal Douglas Haig from heart failure, his funeral procession journeyed through the streets of London. Thousands of former soldiers, and widows and children of soldiers, lined the route to pay their respects to this leader, showing the high esteem in which he was held by the many who served under him.

Although Haig is most famous for his wartime service as Commander-in-Chief of the troops during the First World War, it should also be remembered that he spent the years after the war until his death working tirelessly on behalf of the soldiers who had served under him, leaving a legacy that survives to this day.

Even before the war had ended, Haig had on numerous occasions expressed concern about the treatment of returning soldiers, especially the wounded, and was very concerned about their future and the hardships they might face. He felt that the government had a responsibility to these men, and that it should look after them.

After the war, Haig often met veterans and came to have a good understanding of the privations and suffering many of them faced. Although there were a number of institutions representing veterans, he could see clearly that a single, united organisation, free from political bias and acting on their behalf, was what was needed to have the influence to get the required support. To this end he was instrumental in persuading a number of ex-service groups to amalgamate and thus The British Legion and The British Legion Scotland were formed in 1921, with Haig as their president. He also established the Haig Fund, which sold poppies and is incorporated into the Royal British Legion.

Not only did Haig work on behalf of veterans at home, but he also helped establish the British Empire Service League, which championed the cause of veterans throughout the Empire. He was appointed Grand President of the League. He was also Chairman of both the United Services Fund, which oversaw the allocation of the profits made from army canteens during the war, and the National Benevolent Committee, which was involved in fundraising as well as the administration of welfare funds.

Haig was not only a figurehead for his many organisations, he also worked tirelessly to further their cause. Describing his funeral, an article published on 4 February 1928 in *The Times* stated: 'In the crowds which lined the route many thousands of people wore Flanders poppies, and this symbol linked with the military significance of a moving ceremony, recognition of the great work of the former Commander-in-Chief for the welfare in civil life of the millions who fought for their country.' It was a moving tribute to a great man.

> *In the crowds which lined the route many thousands of people wore Flanders poppies, and this symbol linked with the military significance of a moving ceremony, recognition of the great work of the former Commander-in-Chief for the welfare in civil life of the millions who fought for their country.*

A formal portrait of Field Marshal Sir Douglas Haig on horseback at Poperinghe in 1917.

AIR COMMODORE ROY WILLIAMSON CHAPPELL

MC

awarded 21 June 1918 • Western Front • RFC

▼ The RFC 'Maternity' pattern officer's tunic. This example belonged to noted First World War ace Captain Albert Ball, a VC recipient with 44 victories, who died in April 1917.

Roy Chappell was a First World War ace who scored 11 kills. He was assigned to the Directorate of Operations and Intelligence in 1929 and became one of the RAF's foremost intelligence experts during the Second World War, his knowledge of the Japanese language and people proving invaluable to the war effort.

Roy Chappell was born in Cheddleton, England, on New Year's Eve 1896. Although he started his military service as a private in the South African Cavalry in December 1915, he soon entered officer training. In 1916 he was commissioned as an officer, trained as a pilot, joined the Royal Flying Corps, and had his first aerial victory, all in less than nine months.

His first kill can be considered remarkable, as not only had Chappell held a pilot's certificate for only two months, but he was also flying the Martinsyde G.100 'Elephant', a fighter-bomber that was well known for its lack of manoeuvrability. He built on his

initial success with another kill while flying the Elephant in March 1917. From May 1917 he spent six months as an instructor at Central Flying School. However, in October of that year, he was again on the front, this time as an acting captain and Flight Commander in No. 41 Squadron. His new plane was the Scout Experimental 5a, a much more agile machine than the Elephant.

During his time with No. 41 Squadron, he made a further nine kills, taking down a large range of enemy aircraft, including Albatros DVs and Fokker DRIs. He was awarded the Military Cross for: 'conspicuous gallantry and devotion to duty. He showed the greatest skill and courage in leading patrols, with the result that during four days' operations the formations which he led destroyed 19 enemy aeroplanes and drove down several others, the fate of which was not observed, owing to the intensity of the fighting. He has destroyed altogether five enemy machines, and has driven down seven others out of control.'

After the war, Chappell gained a permanent commission in the RAF as a Flight Lieutenant and after a number of Flight Commander postings, he attended the School of Oriental Studies in 1925 and became Language Officer at the British Embassy in Tokyo later that year.

The year 1929 was to be a significant one in Roy Chappell's life because it saw his first assignment to the Directorate of Operations and Intelligence, an area on which he would focus in the years to come. Although famous for his daring exploits during the First World War, Chappell's contribution to the war effort during the Second World War was also significant. Having spent many of the interwar years posted to Japan, he was made Deputy Director of Intelligence in September 1939, and Director of Intelligence in October 1942. He retired from the RAF after the war in September 1946. Roy Chappell died on 7 February 1982 at the age of 86.

" ... conspicuous gallantry and devotion to duty. He showed the greatest skill and courage in leading patrols, with the result that during four days' operations the formations which he led destroyed 19 enemy aeroplanes and drove down several others, the fate of which was not observed, owing to the intensity of the fighting. He has destroyed altogether five enemy machines, and has driven down seven others out of control. "

The Martinsyde G.100 'Elephant' was a fighter-bomber introduced into service in the summer of 1916. It was large and unwieldy and unsuited to the fighter role, making Roy Chappell's achievements in it even more impressive.

GROUP CAPTAIN OLIVER CAMPBELL BRYSON
OM, GC, MC, DFC WITH BAR

awarded (MC) 5 July 1918 • Western Front • RAF

Oliver Campbell Bryson was an RAF officer and ace who served his country during both World Wars. He was awarded the Order of Merit, Military Cross, Distinguished Flying Cross with Bar, and George Cross for his gallantry both in action and at home.

▼ *The Sopwith 7F.1 Snipe was introduced late in the war and saw service with only a couple of squadrons. Nevertheless, it was involved in a significant number of aerial victories in its short combat history. It saw considerable service in the Allied intervention in North Russia, and was the standard single-seater fighter used by the RAF until its retirement from service in 1926.*

By the time Oliver Bryson was awarded a Bar to his DFC for his role in the action on the Northwestern Frontier of India in 1930, he was already the recipient of not one but three gallantry awards. He had already fought on the Western Front, in the Russian Civil War and in the skies over colonial India.

He was educated at Bromsgrove School and joined the Army in 1914. In 1915, while serving with the Dorset Yeomanry Cavalry in Egypt, he transferred to the Royal Flying Corps. He went on to become an ace with 12 kills to his name, 11 of which were achieved in the final few months of 1917 while flying a SPAD for 19 Squadron in France. He was awarded the MC in July 1918 for 'conspicuous gallantry and devotion to duty'. He 'made several difficult flights in most unfavourable weather, and destroyed several hostile machines. He proved himself a determined and undaunted leader, and set a splendid example of courage on all occasions.'

In 1918, Bryson was also awarded the Albert Medal (an honour that was later replaced by the GC) for rescuing a comrade from a burning plane, despite being injured himself. His citation states: 'On the 15th March 1917, Captain (then Lieutenant) Bryson, with Second Lieutenant Hillebrandt as passenger, was piloting an aeroplane at Wye Aerodrome when, owing to a sideslip, the machine crashed to the ground and

burst into flames. On disentangling himself from the burning wreckage Captain Bryson at once went back into the flames, dragged Lieutenant Hillebrandt from the machine and, notwithstanding his own injuries, which were undoubtedly aggravated by his gallant efforts to rescue his brother officer from the fire, endeavoured to extinguish the fire on Lieutenant Hillebrandt's clothing. Lieutenant Hillebrandt succumbed to his injuries a few days later.'

Following the First World War, Oliver Bryson was sent to Russia in 1919 to support the White Army. It was there that he was awarded the DFC for his part in the perilous missions over the Dwina and Pinega rivers, where he 'flew a Snipe machine with exceptional skill and daring' and was considered a 'very gallant officer [who] proved himself during these exceptionally difficult aerial operations'.

After being stationed in India from 1928 to 1931, Bryson was posted to Central Flying School. He retired from the RAF in 1943 with the rank of Group Captain, after 28 years of distinguished service. A great man who personified his school's motto, *Deo Regi Vicino* (For God, For King, For Neighbour), Oliver Bryson died on 27 March 1977.

> " On disentangling himself from the burning wreckage Captain Bryson at once went back into the flames, dragged Lieutenant Hillebrandt from the machine and, notwithstanding his own injuries, which were undoubtedly aggravated by his gallant efforts to rescue his brother officer from the fire, endeavoured to extinguish the fire on Lieutenant Hillebrandt's clothing. Lieutenant Hillebrandt succumbed to his injuries a few days later. "

CHAPTER TWO

The Legion in peace and war

▼ *The famous cartoon character 'Old Bill' – created by the artist Bruce Bairnsfeather when he served in the trenches in the First World War – was used by the Legion to promote membership.*

I've joined the British Legion. Have you?

The 1930s saw the Legion firmly embedded in British political and social life. The number of members and branches grew, with 3500 branches by 1930, and over 4000 by 1940. Its leadership also changed during the period. After the death of Earl Haig in 1928, another pivotal commander of the First World War, the Earl Jellicoe – who led the British Grand Fleet at the battle of Jutland in 1916 and was described by Winston Churchill as 'the only man on either side who could lose the war in an afternoon' – became president, a role he occupied until he fell ill in 1931, resigning in 1932. Major General Sir Frederick Maurice then took up the role, having been involved in the Legion since its earliest days, and held the position for the next 14 years.

The role of the Legion in providing help for its members and the wider population of ex-servicemen was never more necessary; the Wall Street Crash of 1929 and the Great Depression that followed saw many struggling with debt, unemployment and poverty. In the early 1930s there were still some half a million survivors of the First World War out of work, and the Legion did its best to help them, not least by setting up employment services, which managed to find jobs for 50,000 men in 1935 alone. The steady growth of the Poppy Appeal throughout the 1920s and 1930s gave the Legion the funds to do this, while the poppy factory – initially set up in the Old Kent Road but moved to Richmond in 1924 – provided jobs for 360 disabled ex-servicemen by the end of 1933.

The 1930s saw a growing international movement of ex-servicemen. Initially links were formed with the Allied powers of the First World War – the French, Imperial and Dominion organisations that flourished, as well as the American Legion – and these links were formalised through the establishment of two international bodies: the Fédération Interalliée des Anciens Combattants and the British Empire Services League. However, as the decade passed, the Legion began to build relationships with the former enemy powers of Austria and Germany. Initially this came in the form of low-level links with individual ex-servicemen's organisations, but by 1935 there was some impetus behind

1931   1932   1933   1934   1935

Resignation of Earl Jellicoe, appointment of Major General Sir Frederick Maurice as President

Legion trip to Germany to promote reconciliation and peace

the links and, perhaps inspired by a speech by the Prince of Wales at the Legion conference in 1935, which spoke of offering the 'hand of friendship' to the former enemies, a high-level delegation accepted offers to visit Austria and Germany in July of that year. This trip was widely publicised by the Nazi authorities in Germany, with the delegation meeting not only the foreign minister, Ribbentrop, and the head of the SS, Himmler, but even Adolf Hitler himself. They were also given a tour of Dachau concentration camp, to show that the conditions were not inhumane. Further visits were planned, but there were protests from within the Legion, particularly from the Jewish members, including the former Senior Jewish Chaplain with the British Forces in France.

By 1938 the political situation had changed to such an extent that the Legion offered its services in the Sudetenland crisis, pledging to provide a 17,000-strong neutral police force to oversee a plebiscite in the area. In the end this force was organised but not deployed, though it serves to illustrate the Legion's importance on the international stage as well as its desire to be a force for peace.

With the policy of appeasement clearly having failed, and Europe drifting steadily towards war, the Legion rose to the fore once more. In 1940 some 50 per cent of Britain's Home Guard were Legion members, while the Women's Section ran mobile canteens for those made homeless by German air attacks.

1936	1937	1938	1939	1940
Abdication of Edward VIII sees George VI assume the throne		Legion organises police force for deployment during the Munich Crisis	Outbreak of war sees the Legion heavily involved in Home Defence	

GROUP CAPTAIN LIONEL REES
VC, OBE, MC, AFC

awarded (VC) 5 August 1916 • Western Front • RFC and RAF

Lionel Rees was a highly decorated First World War fighter ace who was awarded the Victoria Cross for a courageous attack on a large German formation in the early hours of the Battle of the Somme on 1 July 1916. He was also a pioneer of aerial archaeology, mapping many of the great Middle Eastern sites. He retired as a group captain in 1931.

Lionel Rees was born and raised in Wales and attended Eastbourne College and the Royal Military Academy at Woolwich. He was commissioned into the Royal Garrison Artillery in 1903 and later served with the West African Frontier Force. Rees had paid for his own flying tuition, and in August 1914 he was seconded to the RFC, initially as an instructor before going

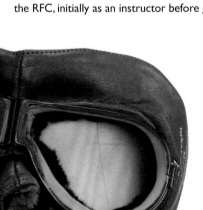

▼ *The Mk I flying mask used by pilots and other aircrew of the RFC and later the RAF.*

on to serve on the Western Front on the Vickers Gunbus with No. 11 Squadron in 1915.

It was with No. 11 Squadron that he received his first award for gallantry, the Military Cross, awarded on 29 October 1915. He was awarded this medal for a series of engagements fought over the summer and autumn of 1915: on 28 July he managed to shoot down a German aircraft despite his machine having been heavily damaged; on 31 August he attacked a much more powerful German aircraft and, despite having to go back to base for more ammunition, he managed to shoot it down; finally, on 21 September he managed to force a quicker and more manoeuvrable German aircraft down, despite being under heavy fire.

Promoted to the rank of major, though only temporarily, he was posted to No. 32 Squadron as its commanding officer in January 1916. Royal Flying Corps support was an integral part of the plan for the British Somme offensive launched on 1 July 1916. In common with many aspects of the plan, the RFC part did not work as desired, with the aircraft unable to provide the support required by the troops below. However, there were successes, as well as losses, as large numbers of British aircraft were put over the front to gain air superiority.

No. 32 Squadron under Rees was one of those committed to the fight. Lee was described by one of his pilots as follows: 'Everyone knows that the major is mad. He is never happier than when he is attacking Huns. I wouldn't be surprised if he comes home with a VC.' His prediction was right. On 1 July 1916 Rees launched his aircraft in the middle of a German formation. Despite being seriously wounded in the leg, a wound that would end his operational career, he scattered the enemy formation, damaging three of them – an act for which he was awarded the VC.

Rees stayed in the RAF in the interwar years, becoming keenly involved in the development of aerial archaeology in the Middle East. He returned to the colours in the Second World War as a wing commander before being invalided out in 1942.

◄ Major Lionel Rees VC, shown when he was the commanding officer of No. 32 Squadron RFC in May 1917.

▼ The Sopwith F1 Camel, one of the most successful aircraft used by the Royal Flying Corps during the First World War.

LIEUTENANT COMMANDER CHRISTOPHER DRAPER

DSC, CROIX DE GUERRE

awarded (DSC) 26 April 1918 • Western Front • RNAS

▼ A Royal Naval Air Service dress jacket. The RNAS was absorbed along with the RFC into the newly formed Royal Air Force on 1 April 1918.

Christopher Draper was a man of many facets. Known as the 'Mad Major', he was a pilot, an ace, a daredevil and a double agent who served during both the First and the Second World Wars. He visited Germany in 1932, which became one of the most significant years of his life.

Christopher Draper was born in 1892. He became interested in aviation in his teens and in 1914 he joined the Royal Naval Air Service (RNAS). In 1916 he was posted to France with No. 3 Naval Wing, flying the 1½ Sopwith Strutter, with which he scored four aerial victories, mainly while on bombing missions over industrial Germany. He then went on to fly for No. 6 Naval Squadron in 1917. He achieved two further aerial victories

during this time, making him an ace. His next plane was the Sopwith Camel, with which he scored three further victories – two while flying for No. 8 Naval Squadron, which he commanded from October 1917, and one after it had become No. 208 Squadron RAF in 1918.

It was towards the end of the First World War that Draper earned the sobriquet 'The Mad Major', as he was known for flying under bridges for the amusement of the troops. He also earned the Distinguished Service Cross and Croix de Guerre for his wartime service.

After the war, Draper had a varied career working as a second-hand-car salesman, a test pilot, a stunt pilot, and finally as an actor. During this time he became more and more disillusioned with the government's treatment of war veterans

◄ HMS *Spurwing* was the RNAS Air Station in Sierra Leone, where Christopher Draper served during the Second World War. This group photo shows all the officers serving on the station.

▼ Sopwith 1½ Strutters of No. 3 Wing at Luxeuil in September 1916. This was the aircraft in which Draper scored his first victories.

and, to raise awareness of the issue (and some say for self-publicity), he flew under two of the bridges over the Thames. This raised his profile and he was invited to join a tour with other First World War aces, which included visiting Germany.

During this visit he met Adolf Hitler – an unlikely meeting for a Merseyside boy, and one that would lead him into a new career as a spy. As his criticism of the government was well known, he was approached by the Nazi party, which wished to use him as an informant. However, he contacted the British authorities on his return and was, in fact, acting as a double agent, giving the Germans false information. He continued for a number of years until the Nazis stopped contacting him.

During the Second World War, Draper joined the Royal Naval Reserve and commanded No. 777 Squadron at Freetown in Sierra Leone, flying anti-submarine missions. After the war he again found it hard to settle into one career and, down on his luck and out of work, in 1953 he decided to recreate his earlier stunt of flying under the Thames bridges. This was again in protest of the government's treatment of veterans, as well as for self-publicity. He managed the amazing feat of flying under 15 bridges at about 90mph (145km/h). Although he was arrested after landing, he was let off with just a fine of the court costs of ten guineas. Christopher Draper died in London in 1979.

MAJOR GENERAL JAMES 'JIMMY' DURRANT

DFC

awarded 7 August 1941 • East Africa • SAAF

▼ *A Douglas Boston aircraft 'S-Sugar' of No. 24 Squadron SAAF running up its engines on an airfield in the North African desert*

Jimmy Durrant was the youngest Allied major general during the Second World War, and joined the South African Air Force (SAAF) in 1934. He commanded squadrons, wings and bomber groups in the Mediterranean theatre from East Africa through the Western desert to the war in Italy. He was awarded the Distinguished Flying Cross for his leadership of No. 40 Squadron SAAF in East Africa in 1940–41.

Jimmy Durrant was born and raised in Johannesburg, South Africa. With the outbreak of the Second World War, he took command of a flight of No. 40 Squadron with the rank of Major, later taking command of the whole squadron.

No. 40 Squadron was equipped with the Hartebees biplane and was used in the ground support role supporting the 1st South African Division during the campaign in East Africa. The South Africans advanced from Kenya into Southern Ethiopia under the British General Alan Cunningham, ably supported by the Hartebees of No. 40 Squadron, and Durrant was awarded the DFC for his flying skills and leadership during the campaign.

The South Africans were moved in 1941 to support the Western Desert Force, with Durrant promoted and taking over command of No. 24 Squadron SAAF, a day bomber squadron equipped initially with Marylands and later Bostons. Durrant commanded this squadron during the bitter fighting in the Western Desert in 1941 and 1942. Promoted again, Durrant took command of No. 3 (SAAF) Bomber Wing, part of the tactical bomber force that prevailed over the battlefields of North Africa and then Sicily and Italy. He took command of

No. 205 Group RAF in 1944, and his group was the one responsible for supplying the fighters of the Polish Home Army when they rose up against the German occupying forces in Warsaw in August 1944. Durrant's force of Liberator bombers, based around Foggia in Italy, had to fly nearly 1000 miles (1600km) each way over hostile territory all the way. Durrant travelled to London to protest that this mission stood little chance of success and would lead to heavy casualties, but Churchill himself told him that the mission had to go ahead. In the event, 39 aircraft were lost in the perilous mission, which did little to prolong the Polish resistance, which ended in October 1944.

Following this, Durrant was promoted to major general and sent to the Far East in command of No. 231 Heavy Bomber Group RAF. He was the youngest major general in the Allied forces at the age of only 32.

Jimmy Durrant remained in the SAAF after the end of the Second World War, becoming Director-General of the Air Force in 1946. He resigned in 1952 following a dispute with the Minister for Defence.

▼ A Consolidated Liberator of No. 205 Group RAF flying between cloud layers, during a supply-dropping mission to Partisan forces in Yugoslavia.

CAPTAIN SIR GEOFFREY DE HAVILLAND
CBE, AFC, OM, FRAᴇS

awarded (CBE) June 1934 • Aircraft designer

▼ The Order of Merit awarded to Geoffrey de Havilland in 1962 at the very end of his illustrious career.

One of the most famous aircraft designers of the twentieth century and creator of so many pivotal British military aircraft, notably the Mosquito of the Second World War, Geoffrey de Havilland was made a Commander of the Order of the British Empire in 1934.

Sir Geoffrey de Havilland was born in 1882 in High Wycombe, Buckinghamshire, and educated in Nuneaton and Oxford. Having trained as an automotive engineer, he was inspired by the pioneers of early flight such as the Wright Brothers; he constructed his first aircraft in 1909. This was a failure, but his second attempt succeeded and was purchased by the British Army's Balloon Factory at Farnborough, Hampshire, in 1911, and de Havilland was taken on as aircraft designer and pilot. This factory later became the Royal Aircraft Factory, with de Havilland joining the Special Reserve of the Royal Flying Corps.

Throughout the First World War de Havilland was responsible for designing many of the aircraft used by both the Royal Flying Corps and the Royal Naval Air Service, as he worked for the Aircraft Manufacturing Company. Following the end of the war, this company was purchased by the Birmingham

Small Arms Company and de Havilland set up on his own, forming the de Havilland Aircraft Company at Edgware in 1920, before moving to Hatfield in 1933.

With his independent company, de Havilland had created the fantastically successful series of Moth biplanes, but it was the Mosquito that was his signature design. Designed from the late 1930s onwards, the Mosquito was an innovative high-speed wooden bomber, originally not intended to carry any defensive armament. The aircraft was introduced into service in 1941 and 7781 were built over a wide range of variants, including bombers, fighter-bombers, photo-reconnaissance and many others. Thanks to its high speed and agility, the Mosquito ended the war with the lowest loss rate of any aircraft in RAF Bomber Command service. It was a unique and much loved plane.

Another success was the first commercial jetliner, the DH-106 Comet, which first flew

Thanks to its high speed and agility, the Mosquito ended the war with the lowest loss rate of any aircraft in RAF Bomber Command service.

◀ *Sir Geoffrey de Havilland in a photo taken in March 1954. Throughout his career he undertook a significant amount of test flying of his own designs.*

in 1951. The de Havilland company was taken over by Hawker Siddely in 1960 and Geoffrey de Havilland's direct connection with the aviation industry ceased. Throughout his career he received many awards for his work; the OBE in 1918, the Air Force Cross in 1919 and the CBE in 1934. He was knighted in 1944 and awarded the Order of Merit in 1962. He died in 1965.

▶ *A Mosquito PR Mark XVI of No. 544 Squadron RAF from Benson, Oxfordshire. The Mosquito was the finest and most famous of Geoffrey de Havilland's designs and was one of the most successful British aircraft of the Second World War.*

ADMIRAL OF THE FLEET JOHN JELLICOE, FIRST EARL JELLICOE

GCB, OM, GCVO

awarded (OM) 31 May 1916 • First World War • Royal Navy

Lord Jellicoe was the commander of the British Grand Fleet for much of the First World War, and the man who led them into action at the Battle of Jutland in 1916. He served as the President of the British Legion from 1928 until 1932.

▶Admiral of the Fleet Sir John Jellicoe, GCB, OM, GCVO, 1918, *by Glyn Philpot RA.*

John Jellicoe was born in 1859 in Southampton. He joined the Royal Navy in 1872 as a cadet, and saw active service on land at the Battle of Tel-el-Kebir in Egypt in 1882, and during the Boxer Rebellion in 1900. Serving as part of Seymour's Naval Brigade, he was shot in the chest and invalided home. In 1905, Jellicoe was called to the Admiralty to become the Director of Naval Ordnance. He was also a member of the committee that oversaw the development and commissioning of HMS *Dreadnought*. In 1907, he was made a rear admiral and knighted, and the following year became Third Sea Lord. In 1911, he became Second Sea Lord. In the month prior to the outbreak of war, he was given the acting rank of admiral and took command of the Grand Fleet based at Scapa Flow.

Jellicoe's cautious approach during the opening years of the war was criticised by those who wanted a major battle against the German High Seas Fleet in the North Sea – a 'new Trafalgar' to win the war. A more aggressive policy was naturally a more risky one; Winston Churchill famously commented that Jellicoe was 'the only man on either side who could lose the war in an afternoon'.

In May 1916, the two fleets met for the only time during the war, in an indecisive encounter at the Battle of Jutland. Although Britain lost more ships, the German fleet sustained greater damage. British claims of victory were perhaps justified by the German decision to stay in port for the remainder of the war. Nevertheless it was no Trafalgar, and Jellicoe was criticised for allowing the High Seas Fleet to escape.

In the aftermath of Jutland, Admiral David Beatty replaced Jellicoe as commander-in-chief of the Grand Fleet. Jellicoe was promoted to First Sea Lord in December 1916, but left office on 24 December 1917 after a serious disagreement with the Prime Minister, David Lloyd George. In 1918 he was made a viscount, and the following year became Admiral of the Fleet. Jellicoe later served as Governor General of New Zealand from 1920 to 1924, and was made an earl.

Following the death in 1928 of the President of the Legion, Earl Haig, Jellicoe was the natural choice as his successor, having been Vice President since 1926. As President he was active and unassuming, taking care to visit as many Legion branches as he possibly could while always concerned to minimise any potential costs to the Legion's purse. He continued in this role until 1932 and died on 20 November 1935. His body was interned beside Nelson's in St Paul's Cathedral, London.

▼ *Battleships of the Grand Fleet cruising in line abreast columns in the North Sea. At the Battle of Jutland on 31 May 1916, Jellicoe deployed the main body of the Grand Fleet from a formation of six columns in line abreast into a single battle line just before the battleships of the German High Seas Fleet came into sight.*

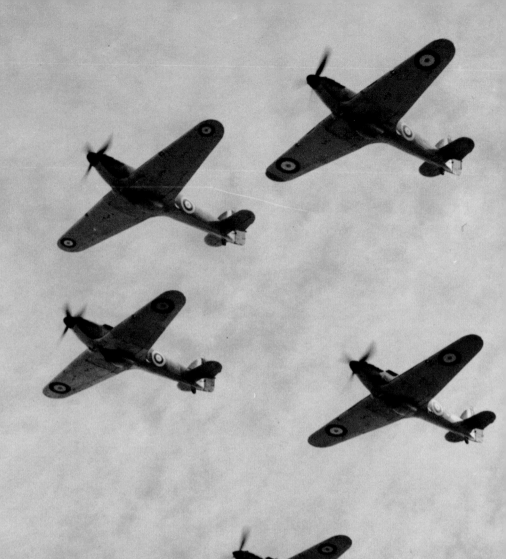

Nine Hawker Hurricanes of No. 85 Squadron RAF shown in
formation in October 1940. Although the Spitfire gained many
of the plaudits, the Hurricane accounted for the majority of RAF
victories during the Battle of Britain.

STAFF SERGEANT WILLIAM COSGROVE
VC, MSM

awarded (VC) 23 August 1915 • Gallipoli • Royal Munster Fusiliers

William Cosgrove was awarded the Victoria Cross for his actions in the early days of the Gallipoli campaign. His was one of six VCs awarded to British forces during the heavily contested landing and its immediate aftermath, and Cosgrove died in 1936, largely due to health problems ensuing from the wounds he received there.

▼ *Corporal William Cosgrove, VC.*

William Cosgrove was a native of Ireland, born in County Cork, and having trained as an apprentice butcher he joined the Royal Munster Fusiliers in 1909. He served in the 1st Battalion, which was posted to Burma, and was recalled to Great Britain in 1915, destined to be committed to the assault on the Gallipoli peninsula.

On 25 April 1915 the invasion force stood off the beaches, with the 1st Royal Munster Fusiliers aboard the SS *River Clyde* going ashore on V Beach, east of Cape Helles.

The British troops were immediately pinned down by heavy fire and unable to reach their target: the village of Sedd-el-Bahr. Around 100 of the 1st Royal Munster Fusiliers were killed or wounded in this first assault. One of the principal obstacles to the breakthrough was the large number of fixed barbed-wire obstacles in their path. The following day it was clear that the assault troops had to push forward and capture the village; otherwise they ran the risk of being eliminated by Turkish shellfire in their exposed beach positions. Corporal Cosgrove was one of a group of men detailed to deal with the mass of barbed wire in front of the British positions. With the officer leading the party killed, Cosgrove took over and led the men forward under heavy fire. They found that the tangle of wires was so thick that their cutters were ineffective, so Cosgrove, a strong man, stood up and started pulling the posts out of the ground with his bare hands. Spurred on by the cheers of his men, he carried on pulling the posts out until the way was clear.

With the barbed wire clear, the advance off V Beach could continue and later in the day Cosgrove was seriously wounded by machine-gun fire, with one bullet going straight through him. He was evacuated from Gallipoli and underwent a series of operations in Malta, but his wounds continued to trouble him until his death in 1936.

Cosgrove stayed in the army after the war, transferring to the Northumberland Fusiliers on the creation of the Irish Free State in 1922. He finally left the army in 1934, after spending six years in Rangoon.

▲ *The landing of the 1st Battalion The Essex Regiment at W Beach, Gallipoli, on 25 April 1915. The landings around Cape Helles were sadly bungled and no breakthrough was possible.*

An Arab Jambiyah with scabbard, taken from a dead Turk at Gallipoli.

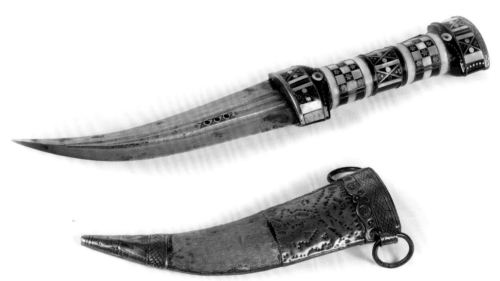

FIELD MARSHAL MONTGOMERY, FIRST VISCOUNT MONTGOMERY OF ALAMEIN
KG, GCB, DSO, PC

▼ Lieutenant General Montgomery as General Officer Commanding 8th Army, watching the beginning of the German retreat from El Alamein from the turret of his Grant Tank in November 1942. He is wearing his famous double-badged tank beret.

awarded (DSO) 1 December 1914 • Western Front • Royal Warwickshire Regiment

---

Bernard Montgomery was the most famous British general of the Second World War, responsible for the victories in the desert as well as the success of the Normandy invasion. He was also awarded the Distinguished Service Order for gallantry during the First World War.

Bernard Montgomery was born in 1887, the son of the Bishop of Tasmania. He attended St Paul's School in London before going up to Sandhurst. In 1908 he was commissioned into the Royal Warwickshire Regiment, with whom he served in the First World War. The 1st Battalion, of which a young Lieutenant Montgomery was part, was thrown into the Battle of Le Cateau on 26 August 1914 during the retreat from Mons. The battalion lost more than half its men, and Montgomery and the men with him survived capture only through hiding by day and marching by night back to the British lines.

Newly promoted to the rank of captain, Montgomery led his troops forward in an attack on German positions near Meteren on 13 October 1914. Mongomery was shot through the lung, and would have died had it not been for a member of his platoon coming up and dressing his wound; his saviour was shot soon afterwards but his body provided a shelter for Montgomery as he lay wounded in no man's land, although he still sustained a further wound in the knee. Despite being so severely wounded that his grave was dug, Montgomery survived, and he was awarded the DSO for his leadership of the attack.

He returned to active service as a staff officer and spent time under Herbert Plumer's command, learning about infantry and artillery cooperation. By the war's end he had risen to the rank of brevet lieutenant colonel. Between the wars, Montgomery served with the British Army of the Rhine in Germany, attended the Army's Staff College in Camberley, and served as a brigade commander in Cork during the Anglo-Irish war. In 1937 he was promoted to brigadier, taking command of 9th Infantry Brigade, and in 1939 he moved to command the 3rd Infantry Division, which saw action in France as part of the British Expeditionary Force (BEF). A succession of corps commands quickly followed after the fall of France, together with promotion to lieutenant general in 1940.

In 1942 Montgomery was appointed to command the 8th Army in North Africa, where his calm, confident and high-profile style of leadership inspired his troops, and he   the decisive battle of the campaign at El Alamein in October–November 1942.

The North African, Italian, Normandy and North-West European campaigns (where Montgomery commanded 21st Army Group) were highly successful for Montgomery, with the exception of the Arnhem operation, and he was promoted to field marshal on 1 September 1944. In 1946 he was invested with the title of First Viscount Montgomery of Alamein. He went on to serve as Chief of the Imperial General Staff and Deputy Supreme Allied Commander Europe, retiring in 1958. He died in 1976.

AIR MARSHAL OWEN BOYD
CB, OBE, MC, AFC

awarded (MC) 19 August 1916 • Western Front • RFC and RAF

▼ *De Havilland DH-4s of No. 27 Squadron RFC. The squadron was equipped with the Martynside G.100 Elephant, and this was the aircraft Owen Boyd flew as a pilot and flight commander on the Western Front in the summer of 1916.*

Owen Boyd was a decorated pilot in the First World War. He was appointed Air Officer Commanding Balloon Command in 1938, went on to high command in the Second World War, and eventually commanded a group in the RAF's Bomber Command.

Owen Boyd started his military career in the Indian Army, having graduated from Sandhurst in 1909. In 1916 he transferred to the Royal Flying Corps (RFC) and served with No. 27 Squadron, flying the unwieldy Martynside G.100 'Elephant'. It was with this squadron that he earned his Military Cross in July 1916 over

the Western Front, and was also promoted to command a flight.

Later in the war he commanded No. 66 Squadron on Sopwith Pups on the Western Front and No. 72 Squadron for what was now the RAF, a mixed unit that was based in Mesopotamia. He moved up the chain of

command in the interwar years, attending Staff College and commanding No. 1 Group RAF, before being appointed Air Officer Commanding Balloon Command. This was a new formation and Boyd was the first commanding officer; its job was to set up a national balloon defence system, with the main focus on protecting London, at least initially. In 1939, 47 Balloon squadrons were set up, deploying fixed barrage balloons designed to put off the aim of enemy bombers, prevent dive-bombing attacks, and keep the attacking formations at a level where they could be targeted by anti-aircraft fire. Boyd remained in charge until 1940, when he was appointed Deputy to the AOC Middle East. However, while he was flying to his new post his aircraft strayed too close to Sicily and was forced down by Italian fighters. Having destroyed their aircraft and any confidential documents, Boyd and his staff were taken prisoner. He was to spend the next three years as a prisoner of war in Italy. He attempted an escape in September 1943 from his prison, the Castle of Vincigliata, near Florence, but was recaptured at Como. However, he made another attempt, along with General Sir Richard Connor and Lieutenant General Sir Philip Neame, which was successful, and he arrived back in Britain in February 1944. After being appointed to command No. 93 Operational Training Unit, he died in August 1944 of a heart attack.

◀ Owen Boyd in 1938, following his promotion to Air Vice Marshal and commander of the newly formed RAF Balloon Command.

▼ Kite balloons and balloon winches of No. 1 Balloon Training Unit are prepared for handling practice at Cardington, Bedfordshire. The barrage balloons deployed by Balloon Command were designed to hinder and break up German bomber formations.

MAJOR ANTHONY BROOKS

DSO, MC, CROIX DE GUERRE, LEGION D'HONNEUR

awarded (DSO) 30 August 1945 • Occupied France • SOE

Tony Brooks joined the Special Operations Executive (SOE) in late 1941 at the age of only 19. He had tried to join the British Army in 1939, but was rejected due to his age. He proved to be a very successful agent in the field, specialising in the sabotage of the French railway network, and went on to serve with the Secret Intelligence Service (SIS) following the end of the war.

▶ *A Lysander Mark IIIA (SD) of No.161 (Special Duties) Squadron RAF on the ground at Tempsford, Bedfordshire. This aircraft was flown on 20 missions to occupied France in 1943 to drop and pick up SOE and Resistance personnel.*

Tony Brooks was living in France at the outbreak of the war and remained there until 1941. Relatives of his were involved in helping British servicemen escape the Continent, and Brooks became involved in this – taking the route himself when he learned the Vichy authorities intended to intern him in May 1941. Escaping over the Pyrenees, Brooks was interned in Spain briefly before going first to Gibraltar and then to England. He applied to work for both MI9 and the SIS but was rejected due to his age – he was only 19 at the time – but he was signed up by the SOE.

Following his training he was parachuted back into France in July 1942, landing near Limoges. Despite being injured in the landing he managed to meet his contacts and establish a network in the region, codenamed Pimento. Following the German occupation of Vichy France in November 1942 this network became more active, receiving regular RAF supply drops, and targeted the French railway network. Returning to England briefly in 1943, he parachuted back into France in December as the pace of resistance activities increased in the run-up to the Normandy invasions.

Brooks' network was responsible for delaying the transport of German forces to the battlefields of Normandy by sabotaging the rail network, managing to disrupt it to the extent that the 2nd SS Panzer Division 'Das Reich' took more than two weeks to travel from Toulouse to Normandy. Brooks had a number of scares during this period, and was arrested and interrogated by the Germans in July 1944, though his cover story held. By August, the German situation had deteriorated so much that Brooks could afford to come out into the open, leading attacks by his network on German transport, and it was for this that he was awarded the Distinguished Service Order in 1945, having already been awarded the Military Cross for his resistance activities.

At the end of the war Brooks transferred to the SIS, leaving in 1952 and rejoining in 1956. He retired in 1977, and passed away in 2007. He was the Honorary Vice President of the Lyon Liberation Branch of the Royal British Legion.

▼ *A photograph taken by Brooks showing Paris during the occupation.*

WING COMMANDER ERIC JAMES BRINDLEY NICOLSON
VC, DFC

awarded (VC) 15 November 1940 • Battle of Britain • RAF

James Nicolson was the only pilot awarded the Victoria Cross during the Battle of Britain. He was awarded the medal for shooting down two German aircraft in August 1940 while his own plane was on fire.

▼ James Nicolson's medal bar, consisting of the Victoria Cross, Distinguished Flying Cross, 1939–1945 Star, Air Crew Europe Star, Burma Star, Defence Medal and War Medal 1939–1945.

James Nicolson was born in London in 1917 and educated at Tonbridge School before becoming an engineer. He joined the pre-war RAF in 1936, joining No. 72 Squadron in 1937 on Gloster Gladiators before moving to No. 249 Squadron

in 1940, which was originally equipped with Spitfires but later changed to Hurricanes.

Nicolson was awarded his VC following an action on 16 August 1940. Nicolson, and other pilots of No. 249 Squadron, had taken off in Hurricanes from RAF Boscombe Down in Wiltshire and were patrolling above Southampton when they were alerted to an incoming German attack. Nicolson engaged a Messerschmitt Bf 110 fighter-bomber, unaware that there were Messerschmitt Bf 109 fighters above. One of these hit his Hurricane with four cannon shells, injuring Nicolson in the foot and head and setting his aircraft on fire. While preparing to bale out of his aircraft Nicolson noticed another Bf 110 nearby and, climbing back into his damaged cockpit, he destroyed it. Only once it was clear that his aircraft was going down in flames did Nicolson bale out, having suffered serious burns in addition to his earlier wounds. On his descent to earth, he was further shot at by members of the Home Guard, who

would not believe that he was an RAF officer. Originally recommended for the DFC, he was upgraded to the VC. His citation is shown on the right.

Nicolson recovered from his wounds and was posted to the Far East, serving as CO of No. 27 Squadron, which flew Bristol Beaufighters over Burma. During this time he was awarded the Distinguished Flying Cross for his work supporting ground forces in the Burma Campaign. Further promoted to wing commander, he was killed on 2 May 1945, when the RAF B-24 Liberator he was travelling in caught fire and crashed into the Bay of Bengal.

> *Flight Lieutenant Nicolson has always displayed great enthusiasm for air fighting and this incident shows that he possesses courage and determination of a high order. By continuing to engage the enemy after he had been wounded and his aircraft set on fire, he displayed exceptional gallantry and disregard for the safety of his own life.*

In a scene rather too obviously set up for the camera, the pilot of a No. 249 Squadron Hurricane looks on as his aircraft is re-armed, North Weald, 28 February 1941.

CHAPTER THREE

1941–1950 The legacies of war

One might have expected the population of Great Britain to be so weighed down by the stresses and strains of the Second World War that their interest and enthusiasm for the casualties and commemoration of the First World War would diminish. However, the opposite was true, with the Poppy Appeal proving to be fantastically successful during the war years, enabling the Legion to invest considerable amounts in capital projects and build up large reserves for the work that they knew was to come.

From the very early days of the war the Legion was keen to ensure that the mistakes made by the government following the end of the First World War should not be repeated after the end of the Second World War, and that provision should be made for those who suffered in the struggle against the Axis powers. The government sought their views and many were put into practice at the end of the war in an attempt to mitigate the problems experienced in the 1920s.

Apart from the vast numbers of the Legion who served in the Home Guard throughout the war, the Legion helped in other practical matters. It represented ex-servicemen who now returned to the colours, thus taking the pivotal step of having a direct involvement in the affairs of current members of HM Armed Forces for the first time. The poppy factory in Richmond was also turned over to essential war work, having already suffered when a German bomb hit the factory's air-raid shelter in 1940, killing eight women and children. The Legion was also very active towards the end of the war in promoting itself to the millions of men and women who served in the armed forces. As a result, following the end of hostilities, there was a vast increase in membership, with numbers up to over a million by 1947, over half of whom were recent veterans of the Second World War. This rise in membership was reflected in the substantial growth in the number of branches, with over 5500 in existence by 1950. Many of the larger branches decided to split, in order to help keep a close connection with their members. These newly formed branches needed accommodation, and the Legion helped in this by providing financial assistance to the ambitious building programme.

◀ A British Legion band marches past beneath portraits of Churchill and Stalin. The marchers were part of a procession of British and allied troops on British-Soviet Red Cross Day.

1941	1942	1943	1944	1945

The Legion becomes involved with active servicemen for the first time

End of the Second World War

▲ Poppies in bloom in June 2008 in Shildon, near Bishop Auckland, County Durham. Photograph taken by Matthey Bradley.

◀ Kippington Court, a country mansion near Sevenoaks, Kent, was given to Winston Churchill by Charles Alfred Hopkins, a London estate dealer, as a mark of his appreciation of Churchill as the 'Architect of Victory'. It was re-named Churchill Court in 1946 when Churchill opened it as a British Legion rehabilitation centre and convalescent home for men who had served in the war.

This vast influx of new members ensured that the Legion would be very busy in what were difficult times for the country. Great Britain struggled in the aftermath of the Second World War; the country had accumulated a vast war debt and rationing remained in force and even increased. To alleviate the hardships of its members, the Legion distributed food parcels sent from well wishers in the empire and dominions, something that would carry on until 1955, while by 1947 benevolent spending had doubled from its level in 1939, and the Legion's involvement in fighting for its members' pension rights had risen from 4000 cases to 32000.

The difficult economic climate also had a massive effect on the Legion's income, which saw a large fall in revenue obtained from the Poppy Appeal: the total gathered from the appeal in 1947 was only half that gathered in 1946, while 1948 and 1949 saw further reductions. The Legion was compelled to dip into its accumulated reserves to the tune of £250,000 in both 1948 and 1949. The birth of the Welfare State in 1948 at least alleviated some of the problems suffered, but it also brought with it new issues related to war pensions, and these were to occupy much of the Legion's time over the following decade.

1946   1947   1948   1949   1950

The Legion has over a million members for the first time

Birth of the Welfare State

Festival of Remembrance first shown on BBC television

COLONEL STUART ARCHER

GC, OBE, ERD

awarded (GC) 30 September 1941 • Bomb Disposal • Royal Engineers

Stuart Archer was awarded the George Cross for his skill and bravery in dealing with unexploded German bombs throughout the Second World War. By the time of his award in 1941, he had already dealt with over 200 unexploded devices. He is now the oldest living recipient of the GC and chairman of the Victoria Cross and George Cross Association.

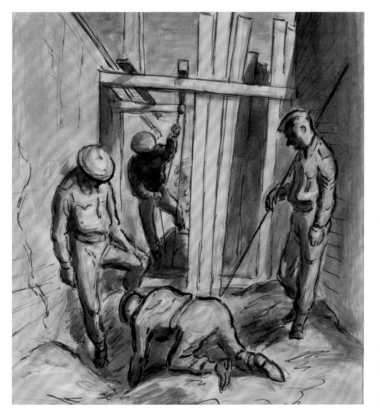

▼ Bomb Disposal Squad: probing for tracks of a bomb in loose earth, *by Edward Ardizzone CBE, RA. Four uniformed soldiers on a bomb site. One is kneeling next to the hole, two others stand around, looking on. The fourth soldier is preparing a winch in the background.*

Stuart Archer was born and brought up in London and qualified as an architect at the age of 21. In 1937 he joined the Honourable Artillery Company, a regiment of the Territorial Army, and in January 1940 he was commissioned into the Royal Engineers and posted to No. 553 Field Company.

He rapidly became something of an expert in the field of bomb disposal, dealing with some 200 bombs before the incident that would cause him to be awarded the GC, including dealing with the first delayed-action fuse at the end of August 1940.

The award of the GC came for a lengthy list of his exploits, culminating in a disposal operation on 2 September 1940, when 2nd Lieutenant Archer was called to the National Oil Refinery at Swansea to deal with some unexploded bombs. The refinery was already on fire following a night of heavy bombing. The unexploded devices were located around the burning oil tanks, with one device directly underneath one of the tanks. Despite the fact that some of the bombs were going off,

Lieutenant Archer dealt with this most difficult bomb first of all. Reaching down to defuse it, he had to carry out most of his work upside down. However, after a tortuous four-and-a-half hours in excruciating heat, with him and his team taking 15-minute shifts, Archer managed to scrape away the fuse and remove it from the bomb. In doing so, he also discovered another mechanism, which turned out to be the Zus anti-handling device that had not worked. Archer removed this as well, the first such device to be successfully retrieved.

Archer finished the war as a lieutenant colonel and returned to his work as an architect. In 1963 he was appointed Honorary Colonel of the bomb disposal regiments of the Royal Engineers, and he has been the Chairman of the Victoria Cross and George Cross Association since 1994. Born on 3 February 1915, Stuart Archer is the oldest surviving recipient of the GC.

▶ *Colonel Stuart Archer GC at a reception at Clarence House in London following a service for the Victoria Cross and George Cross Association reunion at St Martin-in-the-Fields, 9 November 2010.*

▼ *A bomb disposal expert defuses a 1200lb (540kg) bomb on 20 September 1940.*

LIEUTENANT COMMANDER EUGENE ESMONDE
VC, DSO

awarded (VC) 3 March 1942 • attack on the *Scharnhorst* and *Gneisenau* • Fleet Air Arm

▼ *A formation of five Fairey Swordfish Mk I aircraft from the Torpedo Training Unit at Gosport.*

Lieutenant Commander Eugene Esmonde was awarded the Victoria Cross posthumously for his courageous actions in attacking the German capital ships *Scharnhorst* and *Gneisenau* in the English Channel on 12 February 1942. The doomed attack on these heavily protected warships caused the loss of all six of the poorly protected Fairey Swordfish aircraft, with great loss of life.

Esmonde had joined the RAF in 1928 on a five-year commission, before transferring to the Fleet Air Arm. Following the end of his term of service he joined Imperial Airways as a pilot, before returning to the Fleet Air Arm with the rank of lieutenant commander on the outbreak of war in 1939.

Having served on both HMS *Courageous* and HMS *Victorious*, he had already been involved in one dramatic feat of naval aviation earlier in the war when he led the 825 Naval Air Squadron attack on the *Bismarck* on 24 May 1941. Pressing home the attack in the face of fierce anti-aircraft fire, Esmonde did not manage to damage the *Bismarck*, which was later hit by a further aerial attack from the *Ark Royal*. This damaged the ship's rudder, enabling the British surface vessels to catch her up and sink her. For his role in the sinking, Esmonde was awarded the Distinguished Service Order on 11 February 1942.

◄ Officers and ratings who were decorated for the part they played in the sinking of the Bismarck, in front of a Fairey Swordfish aircraft. Lieutenant Commander Eugene Esmonde is second from the left. February 1942.

▼ The German battleships Scharnhorst and Gneisenau travel in a line with their guns firing; a photograph allegedly taken during their escape from Brest, known as the 'Channel Dash', on 12 February 1942.

Later posted to the *Ark Royal*, he was serving aboard her when she was sunk in the Mediterranean in November 1941 and Esmonde was rebuilding the remnants of his squadron on the south coast when the news of the German ships' breakout from the French port of Brest came through.

The Germans planned to move three of their largest capital ships – the battleships *Scharnhorst* and *Gneisenau* and the heavy cruiser *Prinz Eugen* – supported by a flotilla of destroyers and other craft, as well as a strong Luftwaffe presence. The British were expecting the Germans to attempt to break through the Channel, but the response was uncoordinated and, in the event, Esmonde's six Fairey Swordfish, supported by fighter aircraft

from the RAF, was all that could be mustered to put a stop to the formidable German force. Esmonde realised that this mission was suicidal, but pressed home his attack anyway.

His official citation reads: 'Undismayed, he led his Squadron on, straight through this inferno of fire, in steady flight towards their target. Almost at once he was shot down, but his Squadron went on to launch a gallant attack, in which at least one torpedo is believed to have struck the German Battle-Cruisers, and from which not one of the six aircraft returned.

His high courage and splendid resolution will live in the traditions of the Royal Navy, and remain for many generations a fine and stirring memory.'

REAR ADMIRAL BASIL GODFREY PLACE

VC, CB, CVO, DSC

awarded 22 February 1944 • attack on the *Tirpitz* • Royal Navy

▼ *Rear Admiral B. C. G. Place, DSC, RN and the crew of X7, one of the midget submarines that made a successful attack on the Tirpitz at Alten Fjord, on the deck of a ship.*

Rear Admiral Place was awarded his Victoria Cross for a dramatic underwater assault on the German battleship the *Tirpitz* in September 1943. This attack failed to sink the German ship, but kept her out of action until 1944.

Godfrey Place was born in 1921 and, having spent most of his childhood in Africa, joined the Navy at the age of 13. He joined the submarine service in 1941 and was an early volunteer for the experimental midget submarine programme, the X-craft.

At the time, the Royal Navy was dealing well with the threat to the Atlantic and Arctic convoys from the U-boats, but remained aware of the destructive power of the vessels of the German surface fleet, notably the battleship *Tirpitz*. The *Tirpitz* had sortied only three times from her Norwegian base, but the threat she offered to convoys, or even a possible invasion force, led to her presence being taken very seriously indeed. The Admiralty resolved to disable or sink the German ship using the X-craft in an assault in September 1943 codenamed Operation Source.

With Place in charge of the four-man crew of X-7, the operation was launched on 20 September, with ten X-craft towed by submarine

to the *Tirpitz*'s base in Norway,. Two were lost on the way, but the remaining eight launched an assault on the *Tirpitz*, with three breaching the surrounding defences and two – X-5 and Place's X-7 – managing to lay their mines.

As the official citation describes: 'To reach the anchorage necessitated the penetration of an enemy minefield and a passage of 50 miles (80km) up the fjord, known to be vigilantly patrolled by the enemy and to be guarded by nets, gun defences and listening posts, this after a passage of at least a thousand miles (1600km) from base. Having successfully eluded all these hazards and entered the fleet anchorage, Lieutenants Place and Cameron, with a complete disregard for danger, worked their

small craft past the close anti-submarine and torpedo nets surrounding the *Tirpitz*, and from a position inside these nets, carried out a cool and determined attack.'

The blast from the mine damaged Place's craft and, with it unmanageable and taking fire from the alerted German ship, Place decided to abandon ship. Surfacing, he surrendered just before his vessel capsized, taking two of the crew with it. The surviving crewmembers spent the rest of the war in captivity.

Following the end of the war, Godfrey Place transferred into the Fleet Air Arm, saw active service in the Korean War, and ended his career as a rear admiral in 1970. He passed away in 1994.

▲ The Wreck of the Tirpitz, June 1945 *by Stephen Bone. Although seriously damaged by both the midget submarine attack on 22 September 1943 and the later bombing raids on 3 April 1944, the Tirpitz was finally sunk by the Royal Air Force using Tallboy bombs dropped from Lancaster bombers on 12 November 1944.*

MAJOR ROBERT HENRY CAIN
VC

awarded 31 October 1944 • Battle of Arnhem • South Staffordshire Regiment

Major Robert Cain was the only survivor of four men awarded the Victoria Cross for their courageous behaviour during the battle of Arnhem, the ill-fated airborne operation launched in September 1944 in an effort to force a crossing over the river Rhine.

▼ The Denison smock worn by British airborne troops. It was named after its designer, Major Denison. The smock was introduced for service in 1941, and comprised a camouflaged, heavy-duty, windproof, jacket-like garment, to be worn over battledress. Late-war versions of the smock were fitted with windproof woollen cuffs.

Robert Cain had served as a Territorial in the Honourable Artillery Company in the pre-war years and on the outbreak of the Second World War he was commissioned into the Royal Northumberland Fusiliers, before transferring into the 2nd Battalion the South Staffordshire Regiment, which was part of the 1st Airborne Division. Having been held in reserve during the Normandy landings, the 1st Airborne Division had its most famous hour at the battle of Arnhem, part of Field Marshal Sir Bernard Montgomery's Operation Market-Garden.

This was a bold plan to drop British, American and Polish troops onto a series of vital river crossings, with armoured columns breaking through the German positions to relieve the lightly equipped airborne forces. The 1st Airborne Division, of which Major Cain was part, was to seize the furthest of these targets – the bridge over the Lower Rhine at Arnhem.

The operation was launched on 17 September, but Major Cain's glider became separated from its tug and was forced to land, and he made it to Arnhem only on the 18th, finally linking up with his company on the 19th. By this point it was clear that the operation was going wrong. The British forces had expected only light resistance and were shocked to find themselves facing strong German forces, including SS troops and armour. Major Cain's company was struggling to break through to the small numbers of British troops who had managed to get to the vital road bridge in Arnhem itself. The lightly armed British troops were equipped with only the PIAT – a hand-held anti-tank weapon – and the South Staffords were overrun, with only Major Cain's company managing to escape and withdraw into the defensive perimeter that was being established

> During the course of the battle Major Cain was responsible for the destruction of some six armoured vehicles and had provided vital leadership.

▲ *A formal portrait of Major Cain taken following the investiture of his VC at Buckingham Palace.*

around the town of Oosterbeek. From 20 to 25 September, Major Cain played a leading role in the defence of this perimeter. He took personal responsibility for dealing with German armour, equipping himself with a PIAT and destroying a German self-propelled gun on 21 September, despite being wounded by falling masonry and machine-gun fire. On the 24th he also managed to put a feared Tiger tank out of action through the use of a 6-pdr anti-tank gun, even though he had suffered further wounds. By 25 September the British had run out of PIAT ammunition, so Major Cain resorted to using a 2-inch mortar at almost point-blank range to drive back the encroaching German forces. That night, the British withdrew, and Major Cain managed to escape across the Lower Rhine with the other survivors. During the course of the battle, Major Cain was responsible for the destruction of some six armoured vehicles and had provided vital leadership in preventing a breakthrough of his section of the Oosterbeek perimeter.

The Bren Mk 2 machine gun. For the lightly armed airborne troops at Arnhem, the Bren was a key source of firepower.

MAJOR ANDERS LASSEN
VC, MC AND TWO BARS

awarded (VC) 4 September 1945 • Lake Comacchio • SBS (Royal Marines)

Major Anders Lassen was posthumously awarded the Victoria Cross for his actions around Lake Comacchio on the night of 8/9 April 1945, when he singlehandedly took on a number of German machine-gun positions.

▼ *Men of 'L' Squadron SBS investigate the ruins of the Acropolis in Athens, 13–14 October 1944.*

Born in 1920 in Denmark, Anders Lassen left for Great Britain after the beginning of the Second World War and enlisted in the Commandos, serving first of all with No. 62 Commando, also known as the Small Scale Raiding Force. This was a small unit jointly controlled by the Special Operations Executive and Combined Operations HQ. It was intended as an amphibious sabotage force to carry out raids along the French coasts and in the Channel Islands, and it was with this unit that Lassen earned the first of his three Military Crosses, as well as field commission.

When 62 Commando was disbanded in 1943, its personnel was transferred to other units, with Lassen ending up in the Special Boat Squadron (SBS) in the Mediterranean under the command of Lieutenant Colonel George Jellicoe. He served with this unit throughout the war in the Mediterranean, taking part in many clandestine actions, and ended up in Italy, where he was to earn the ultimate award for valour.

On the night of 8/9 April, Lassen – who was by this time a major – was sent along with another officer and 17 men to launch a diversionary attack on the north shore of Lake Comacchio in order to draw German attention away from a major assault on the western side of the lake. Having paddled across the lake, Lassen and his men found themselves on a narrow road surrounded by water on both sides when they were challenged and the enemy

By his magnificent leadership and complete disregard for his personal safety, Major Lassen had, in the face of overwhelming superiority, achieved his objectives.

▲ *Major Anders Lassen, recipient of the Victoria Cross at Lake Commachio, Italy, on 8 April 1945.*

▶ *Corporal Aubrey of the SBS sharpens his fighting knife as he prepares for combat in the Mediterranean. Lassen fought with the SBS throughout many of their actions in the Mediterranean.*

opened fire from dead ahead, as well as from a series of machine-gun pillboxes that covered the causeway. Lassen immediately ran forward and eliminated the first position, before moving on to the next, which he attacked with grenades, silencing it. He was moving towards the third positions when, believing it to be surrendering, he revealed himself and was mortally wounded by a burst of machine-gun fire.

The closing words of his official citation read: 'By his magnificent leadership and complete disregard for his personal safety, Major Lassen had, in the face of overwhelming superiority, achieved his objectives. Three positions were wiped out, accounting for six machine guns, killing eight and wounding others of the enemy, and two prisoners were taken. The high sense of devotion to duty and the esteem in which he was held by the men he led, added to his own magnificent courage, enabled Major Lassen to carry out all the tasks he had been given with complete success.'

Two British soldiers on patrol in the ruins of the Burmese town of Bahe during the advance on Mandalay in January 1945. The campaign in Burma by Fourteenth Army was the longest single campaign of the Second World War.

NANCY WAKE

AC, GM

awarded 17 July 1945 • Occupied France • SOE

Nicknamed the 'White Mouse' by the Gestapo, Nancy Wake was the most wanted resistance fighter in Occupied France in the early years of the war. She escaped to England, was trained by the Special Operations Executive (SOE) and parachuted back into France, and was heavily involved in the build-up to D-Day.

Born in New Zealand and brought up in Australia, Nancy Wake led an adventurous life from an early age. She ran away from home at the age of 16, and later travelled to New York and London, where she trained as a journalist, before settling in Paris as a European correspondent for Hearst newspapers. In 1939 she married the French industrialist Henri Fiocca and the couple moved to Marseille. With the outbreak of war and the fall of France, Wake became involved in resistance activities, helping to run the escape network set up by Captain Ian Garrow to assist British airmen and soldiers stranded in France. In the course of these activities she attracted more and more attention from the Vichy and German authorities until, following the betrayal of the network in December 1943, she was forced to flee from France, making six attempts to cross the Pyrenees before she finally succeeded.

Recruited by SOE, she was trained in Morse code, radio operation and the other skills necessary to her trade, and was parachuted back into France in April 1944, based in the Auvergne region. By this point the resistance was increasing the pace of its activities in the run-up to the invasion of Normandy, and Nancy Wake was responsible for organising countless weapons resupply trips by the RAF in her role as the connection between the local resistance fighters and London. She also took part in resistance activity, leading attacks on German positions including the Gestapo HQ in Montluçon; in the course of one of these raids, she killed a sentry with her bare hands. Following the end of the war, Wake was awarded the George Medal, the US Presidential Medal of Freedom, the Médaille de la Résistance, and the Croix de Guerre. She also discovered that her husband had been captured by the Germans in 1943, tortured and then executed. Remaining in intelligence, she worked for the British Air Ministry in the 1950s before returning with hew new husband to Australia, where she tried to enter politics. Returing to London in 2001, Nancy Wake now lives in the Royal Star and Garter Home for ex-servicemen in Richmond.

◄ Nancy Wake shown in the uniform of the First Aid Nursing Yeomanry (FANY), into which she was commissioned prior to being parachuted into France in April 1944.

▼ A member of the French Forces of the Interior (FFI) uses a truck for cover during gun battles with German snipers in Dreux, August 1944. During this period, several French towns were liberated by the FFI in advance of Allied forces.

CAPTAIN LIONEL MATTHEWS
GC, MC

awarded (GC) 28 November 1947 • Borneo • 8th Australian Division Signals

As a prisoner of the Japanese following the fall of Singapore, Lionel Matthews directed an underground military organisation and, following its discovery, refused to give up the names of his colleagues and was executed by the Japanese. For his heroic behaviour he was awarded the George Cross.

▼ *Emaciated British prisoners in a Japanese prisoner-of-war hospital at Nakom Paton, Thailand, in 1945.*

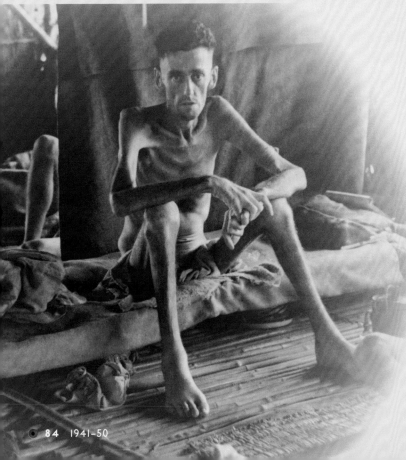

Matthews was born and brought up in the city of Adelaide, South Australia, and was commissioned as a signals lieutenant in the militia in January 1940. He entered the Australian Imperial Force in June 1940 and was posted to the 8th Australian Division, with whom he spent seven months training before the division embarked for Singapore, where they arrived in February 1941.

With the outbreak of the war in the Far East on 8 December 1941, Matthews and the men of the 8th Australian Division were heavily involved in the fighting, with Matthews being awarded the Military Cross (posthumously) for his role in maintaining cable communications both at Gemas in Malaysia and in besieged Singapore itself during January and February 1942; he was also promoted to captain at this time.

With the fall of Singapore on 15 February, Matthews was first interned in Changi Prison, before being shipped along with 1496 other Australians to Sandakan, North Borneo, in July 1942. Here Matthews set about establishing an elaborate intelligence network, making contact with local European officials and internees, as

well as Chinese and other local officials who had belonged to the British North Borneo Constabulary. Through this, Matthews managed to obtain a revolver, maps, information, medical supplies and parts for a wireless receiver. Matthews extended his network to the extent that he made contact with Filipino guerrillas operating in the Sulu Archipelago and enabled parties of Australian prisoners to escape. In January 1943, when the civilian internees were removed from Borneo, Matthews was even placed in charge of the armed constabulary, preparing them to take part in an uprising should the allies land on Borneo.

However, in July 1943 the Japanese captured and tortured four Chinese members of his organisation and they gave up Matthews' name. He was arrested, interrogated, tortured and deprived of food. Sentenced to death, Matthews was executed by firing squad on 2 March 1944 at Kuching, where he was buried.

His achievements in such difficult circumstances were summed up in the official citation for his GC, awarded in 1947 (see above right).

▲ *Studio portrait of Captain Lionel Matthews GC, MC, 8th Australian Division Signals.*

▶ Orderly on his rounds in X Ward, Changi Gaol, Singapore, with POWs suffering from starvation and Beri-Beri, *by Leslie Cole (oil on canvas, 1945).*

" He displayed the greatest gallantry in circumstances of the gravest danger. His leadership conduct, unflagging optimism and imperturbability were an inspiration to all closely associated with him in the resistance organisation and to his fellow prisoners … His conduct at all times was that of a very brave and courageous gentleman and he worthily upheld the highest traditions of an Australian Officer.' "

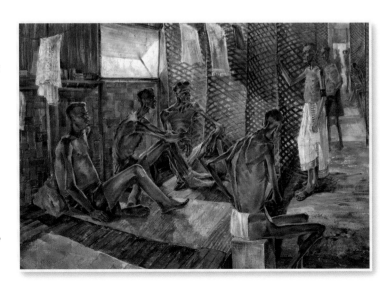

SQUADRON LEADER NORMAN WILLIAMS
CGM, DFM AND BAR

awarded (CGM) 6 July 1943 • Occupied Europe • RAAF

1948

▼ *Aerial photograph taken during a daylight attack on German warships docked at Brest, France. Two Handley Page Halifaxes of No. 35 Squadron RAF fly towards the dry docks in which the battleships Scharnhorst and Gneisenau were berthed in December 1941.*

Norman Williams ended the war as the most decorated airman of the Royal Australian Air Force (RAAF), as well as the only non-fighter ace, having been responsible for shooting down eight German planes and badly damaging three or four others from his position as a rear gunner. It was in this role that he earned the Conspicuous Gallantry Medal in June 1943. He left the RAAF in 1948 as a flight lieutenant.

Norman Williams was born and brought up in New South Wales, Australia, and joined the Australian Army before transferring rapidly to the Air Force in May 1941. Coming top of his course as an air gunner, he was shipped over to England where he became the rear gunner on a Halifax bomber of No. 10 Squadron RAF, based in Yorkshire, where he served a tour of 30 missions bombing Germany and occupied Europe by night. Over the course of this tour, Williams was awarded both the Distinguished Flying Medal and Bar. With the completion of his tour, the whole of Williams' crew volunteered to serve with No. 35 Squadron RAF, which was a Pathfinder squadron that flew ahead of the main bombing force to mark the target.

It was while serving with this squadron that Williams earned his CGM on the night of 11/12 June 1943 during a raid on the German city of Düsseldorf. William's Halifax had come under attack by two night-fighters and been severely damaged: one of the wings was on fire and the rear turret containing Williams was badly smashed, with Williams at first thinking one of his legs had been blown off. The rest of the crew was preparing to bale out.

Despite the severity of his wounds – he was paralysed down one side below the waist, with a cannon shell wound to his stomach and several machine-gun wounds to his legs – Williams shouted at his pilot to turn to starboard and he shot down an approaching German fighter, a feat he repeated a second time when another night-fighter attacked the damaged Halifax when it had managed to drop its bombload. The crippled plane was forced to fly at low-altitude over occupied Europe, a target for flak all the way, before crash-landing in England. Williams had to be cut from the aircraft and spent several months in hospital. King George VI pinned the CGM on him at a private investiture at Buckingham Palace – and the two later shared a bottle of beer.

Williams returned to Australia in 1944, serving as a belly gunner on a Liberator in No. 23 Squadron RAAF. He was recalled to the colours in 1952 for service in the Malayan Emergency and Korean War.

▶ Royal Australian Air Force, Bomber Command, Pathfinder Force, No. 35 Squadron; 411624 Flight Sergeant (later Squadron Leader) Norman Francis Williams, CGM, DFM and Bar, air gunner 35 Sqdn, RAF, Essendon; *painted by Roy Rousel in Australia in 1957.*

▼ *A Halifax Mk II Series 1 of No. 35 Squadron RAF, on the ground at Linton-on-Ouse, Yorkshire. As a Pathfinder squadron, the aircraft of No. 35 Squadron would be in the forefront of any bombing attacks.*

NOOR INAYAT KHAN

GC, MBE, CROIX DE GUERRE

awarded 5 April 1949 • Occupied France • SOE

Noor Inayat Khan was the first woman radio operator smuggled into Occupied France to form a vital link between the Special Operations Executive (SOE) and the French Resistance. Operating in highly perilous circumstances for three-and-a-half months before she was captured. She refused to reveal any details of her resistance activities, and this, coupled with her undaunted spirit in the face of her eventual execution, led to the award of the George Cross posthumously in 1949.

▼ *The liberation of Dachau Concentration Camps. Inmates greet American soldiers in April 1945.*

Noor Inayat Khan had an exotic background: descended from the famous Tipu Sultan, the eighteenth-century ruler of Mysore, she was born in Moscow and raised in London and France, where she was educated at the Sorbonne and the Paris Conservatoire, before writing children's books for a living. On the outbreak of the Second World War, she trained as a nurse before fleeing with her family to Great Britain. Here she volunteered for service with the Women's Auxiliary Air Force (WAAF) in November 1940 and was trained as a wireless operator.

At this stage of the war the SOE was desperate for those with the requisite language skills, and a fluent French speaker such as Noor was perfect for them. She transferred to F Section of the SOE in February 1943, with the cover story of moving to the FANY. Following her training she became the first radio operator to be flown into Occupied France on 16 June 1943. She made contact with the French

◄ Noor Inayat Khan shown in the uniform of the WAAF. She transferred to F Section of the SOE in February 1943 and was the first woman wireless operator to be sent to France on the night of 16/17 June 1943.

'Prosper' resistance network in Paris and was their only link to London when all the other radio operators were captured following a Gestapo crackdown.

Despite being given the option of returning to Great Britain because of the danger of her task, she remained in Paris until her eventual betrayal in October 1943. Initially held in Gestapo headquarters in Paris, she was transferred to Germany following a series of escape attempts. Held first at Pforzheim prison, she was eventually moved to Dachau concentration camp, where she was executed on 12 September 1944. Throughout her incarceration she was repeatedly interrogated but refused to reveal any details of her work for SOE.

Immediately after the end of the war she was awarded a Mention in dispatches and the French Croix de Guerre with Gold Star, and in 1949 came the award of the GC, with the citation emphasising that she 'displayed the most conspicuous courage, both moral and physical, over a period of more than 12 months'.

A Webley 6.35mm pocket pistol associated with Noor Inayat Khan. The pistol was preserved by her brother.

MAJOR KENNETH MUIR
VC

awarded 5 January 1951 • Korea • Argyll and Sutherland Highlanders

▼ *Centurion tanks and men of the Gloucestershire Regiment advance towards Hill 327 in Korea in February 1951.*

Kenneth Muir was a recipient of one of the four Victoria Crosses to be awarded to British troops for actions in the Korean War. His posthumous award was for his outstanding leadership in the struggle for a position known as Hill 282 during the UN forces' advance from the Pusan perimeter to link up with the amphibious landings at Inchon.

◀ *A portrait of Major Kenneth Muir, The Argyll and Sutherland Highlanders.*

▼ *The Korea Medal, the British Commonwealth campaign medal for the war.*

Following the sudden North Korean onslaught on 25 June 1950, South Korean forces were pushed back and the capital Seoul lost. Only the immediate arrival of a small numbers of US forces prevented the country from collapsing completely. The remaining troops, now under the authority of the UN, were clustered into a defensive pocket in the far south-east of the country, based around Pusan.

British and Commonwealth troops – originally grouped in independent brigades but later organised into the Commonwealth Division – were among the first UN troops to arrive in theatre, with land forces in the form of 27th Infantry Brigade disembarking at Pusan on 28 August 1950. Among the first British troops to arrive were men of the Argyll and Sutherland Highlanders and the Middlesex Regiment, and they were soon involved in the fighting in the breakout from Pusan, which pushed the North Korean forces into retreat.

The Argylls were tasked with taking a North Korean position called Hill 282 with two companies, which they successfully managed on the morning of 23 September 1950. Major Kenneth Muir was the battalion second-in-command and came up with stretcher bearers to evacuate the wounded from the original attack. Finding the position under counterattack by North Korean forces, who were shelling and mortaring it as well as infiltrating around the flanks, he remained on the summit and grouped the two companies together into a single force under his command.

An airstrike was called up to drive back the North Koreans, but this was misplaced and caused severe casualties among the Argylls, forcing them off the crest of the hill. Reorganising what remained of his men, Major Muir led them back up to the summit under heavy fire. Having run out of ammunition for his gun, Major Muir then operated a 2-inch mortar until he was mortally wounded by enemy fire. Even then Major Muir carried on encouraging the Argylls to stand firm and not be driven off the hill. Major Muir was awarded the VC posthumously for his bravery, with the citation stating that 'it was entirely due to his magnificent courage and example and the spirit which he imbued in those about him that all wounded were evacuated from the hill'.

CHAPTER FOUR

The struggle for pensions

Although the Legion was to remain deeply involved in the welfare of its members and the struggle for their rights throughout the 1950s, it also retained its principal role in Remembrance and the commemoration of the two world wars. In 1945 it had been decided that the focus of these commemorations would be the closest Sunday to 11 November, which became known as Remembrance Sunday. By coincidence, in 1945 (the year the change was made) this Sunday was also the 11th. Remembrance Sunday would now see the great ceremonies at the Cenotaph and other war memorials throughout the country, while the Legion's Festival of Remembrance, which was held at the Albert Hall, continued to attract the support of royalty; it was listened to by millions on BBC radio and, from 1950, it was shown on television as well. Although the years of separation

▼ *Standard bearers of the Legion on parade at the Royal Military Academy, Sandhurst, in 1958. The bearers wear the medals of both world wars.*

between the tumultuous events of 11 November 1918 inevitably loosened the link between the general population and the remembrance of the First World War, by 1957 the Festival of Remembrance was still the third most popular broadcast on the BBC after those other great bastions of British life: the Queen's Christmas broadcast and the Cup Final.

It was now the Queen's Speech, as King George VI, worn out after his wartime exertions, had passed away in 1952. The Legion played an important role in his successor's coronation, with some 55 of the Legion's standards taking part in the coronation procession, and 40 000 legionaries parading in a royal review. To the delight of the Legion, the new Queen agreed to become patron of the organisation.

The 1950s also saw the Legion deeply embroiled in the thorny issue of war pensions. The rise in inflation and living costs was eroding the value of these awards, with war widows potentially receiving less than ordinary widows might receive, while a miner would receive more for a disability than an ex-serviceman would. Although many in government were quite happy to run down the value of war pensions and allow the slack to be taken up by the other provisions of the

1951	1952	1953	1954	1955
The Legion launches a major campaign for improved War Pensions	Death of King George VI	The coronation of Queen Elizabeth II		

Coronation Edition

VOL 33. No. 6. JUNE

FOURPENCE

BRITISH LEGION JOURNAL

C II R

welfare state, the Legion was keen to emphasise the uniqueness of the contribution required for a war pension, the notion of service and sacrifice that was at the core of what the Legion represented. This campaign for an increase was a partial success, with the government approving a rise in the level of pensions in 1954. But it was not as much as the Legion was calling for, and the struggle was to continue into the 1960s.

These campaigns cost money, and the Poppy Appeal still struggled throughout the early 1950s. In 1960 the Legion was forced to take a bank overdraft in order to carry on its benevolent and other activities. This was partly a generational issue, which the Legion needed to address. Many of the Poppy collectors were from the earliest generation of Legion volunteers and were now growing old, with not so many from the younger generation coming through to replace them. This was reflected in the Legion's membership in general, as it was finding it difficult to attract National Servicemen, who were less enthused by their military service and less inclined to dwell on it in later life. The 1960s would see strenuous efforts by the Legion to attract new blood into the organisation and appeal to these new veterans.

1956

1957

1958

1959

1960

The centenary of the Victoria Cross, with the Legion helping to organise celebrations

Major memorials unveiled at Cassino and Dunkirk with strong Legion participation

SERGEANT WILLIAM SPEAKMAN
VC

awarded 25 December 1951 • Korea • King's Own Scottish Borderers

Nicknamed the 'Beer Bottle VC', Private William Speakman earned his Victoria Cross during a hard-fought battle in Korea on 4 November 1951.

▼ *Sergeant William Speakman, VC, from the 1st Battalion KOSB, looking at grave markers in the UN cemetery in Pusan, after the Commemoration Parade on 12 August 1952.*

Born in 1927, Bill Speakman joined the Black Watch, having served as a drummer in the Army Cadet Corps in his home town of Altrincham, Cheshire. Aged 24, he was attached to the 1st Battalion The King's Own Scottish Borderers (KOSB) and was sent to Korea in 1951.

In October 1951 the United Nation forces in Korea, under General James Van Fleet, began a new phase of offensive operations known as Operation Commando, which was intended to advance UN positions some ten miles (16km) north of the 38th Parallel, the disputed borderline between North and South Korea. In an area overlooking the Imjin River, British Commonwealth forces were tasked with taking a series of hills occupied by Chinese Communist troops, notably Kowang-San (Hill 355) and Maryang San (Hill 317).

As part of the first phase of attacks, the KOSB followed their piper up the western face of Kowang-San and drove out the Chinese occupants on 4 October 1951. Nearby, Australian troops faced serious resistance, but, after five days of fighting, they captured Hill 317 and were relieved in their positions by the Borderers.

The Borderers held the positions for a month until 4 November, when the Chinese counter-attacked in an effort to retake the hills. The KOSB found themselves under a relentless

barrage of shell and mortar fire for 12 hours until, at 1615 hours, Chinese infantry began to advance, engaging the Borderers in fierce close-quarter fighting. By 1730 hours the Chinese had overrun the high point of the hill, and destroyed the forward defences of B Company, but the rest of the unit remained largely in position.

At this point, Private Speakman learnt that B Company's NCOs were wounded, and he took the initiative. He gathered up a large pile of grenades and led a party of six men in ten grenade charges against the enemy, somehow ignoring their withering machine gun and mortar fire. With great courage, he continued to lead charges against the enemy that resulted, in the words of the *London Gazette*, 'in an ever-mounting pile of enemy dead'.

Almost inevitably, Speakman was wounded in the leg, and only after a direct order did he retire to have his wound dressed. He reappeared to lead yet more attacks against the Chinese infantry, before his company finally withdrew at

2100 hours. Subsequent reports state that as the ammunition diminished, Speakman began lobbing anything he could find at the enemy, including beer bottles, but he kept the enemy at bay long enough for his company to withdraw safely. 'His great gallantry and utter contempt for his own personal safety were an inspiration to all his comrades.'

The Chinese finally withdrew, and intelligence later showed that the 1st Battalion had been attacked by an entire infantry division of 6000 men, at least 1000 of whom were killed, against KOSB losses of 31 killed, 90 wounded and 20 captured.

Private Speakman was repatriated and became the first VC to receive his award from Queen Elizabeth II, on 27 February 1952. He went on to serve in Borneo, Radfan and Malaya, achieving the rank of sergeant and later serving with the SAS.

▼ *Two men of the 1st Battalion The Black Watch relax before moving off on patrol in Korea in 1952.*

FLIGHT LIEUTENANT JOHN QUINTON

GC, DFC

awarded 23 October 1951 • Catterick, Yorkshire • RAF

Flight Lieutenant Jon Quinton was a night-fighter navigator and a veteran of the Second World War. He died in a training accident in 1951, sacrificing his life for that of a young air cadet, and was posthumously awarded the George Cross for his actions.

▼ *The Vickers Wellington Bomber Mk I entered RAF service in 1938 and was retired in 1953. Over 11000 were built – more than any other British aircraft during the Second World War.*

John Quinton was undoubtedly a man who loved flying. Born in London in 1921, he joined the Specialoids engineering company in 1937, and, because the company carried out vital war work, Quinton was exempt from being called-up. In 1941, however, he joined the Royal Air Force as a navigator, in order to contribute more directly to the war effort. Quinton applied the same dedication to his RAF career as he had done to the exacting work at Specialoids, learning to navigate in night fighters. He was commissioned in January 1942 and flew Mosquitoes with No. 604 Squadron, notably taking part in the destruction of two Junkers and a Dornier on 2/3 July 1944 over Normandy with Wing Commander Michael Constable-Maxwell, for which he was awarded the Distinguished Flying Cross.

Quinton was promoted and served in the Far East, ending the war as a flight commander. When he was demobbed, he returned to his old job, got married and had a baby, but he missed flying and in 1951 he rejoined the RAF at 228 Operational Conversion Unit, reverting to the rank of flight lieutenant and embarking on a refresher course.

On 13 August 1951 Quinton was a navigator under instruction in a Wellington bomber when it was involved in a mid-air collision with a Martinet training aircraft. The Wellington broke up under the force of the impact and began to spiral out of control towards the ground. Quinton and a 16-year-old air cadet, Derek Coates, were in the observation bubble of the aircraft. Parachutes for the crew were stowed on board in the rear of the aircraft and crew wore harnesses so that parachutes could be clipped on quickly if needed. In the observation astrodome, there was only one parachute and as the aircraft hurtled toward earth, Flight Lieutenant Quinton clipped it on to Air Cadet Coates' chest. He gestured to show him how to pull the ripcord, then pushed him out of the plane. Coates landed safely, but Quinton and the six other members of the crew died when the plane crashed in fields near Catterick.

Derek Coates was the sole survivor and he knew that he owed his life to John Quinton. Quinton was posthumously awarded the GC, which was presented to his widow in the first investiture of Elizabeth II's reign, on 27 February 1952.

Quinton's extraordinary sacrifice has not been forgotten by the RAF. The Quinton Memorial Trophy is awarded annually to the NCO that gains the highest results at Cranwell, the RAF training college, and in 2002 the new squadron headquarters of the Middlesborough Air Training Corps was dedicated to his memory.

> Flight Lieutenant Quinton acted with superhuman speed, displaying the most commendable courage and self-sacrifice, as he well knew that in giving up the only parachute within reach he was forfeiting any chance of saving his own life. (London Gazette, 23 October 1951)

REAR ADMIRAL STANLEY 'MAC' McARDLE
CB, MVO, GM

awarded (GM) 6 October 1953 • Irish Sea • Royal Navy

Rear Admiral 'Mac' McArdle was a career officer in the Royal Navy who risked his own life in the stormy waters of the Irish Sea to rescue passengers from a stricken car ferry in January 1953.

▼ HMS Contest was a Co-Class Destroyer commissioned in 1942 and the first Royal Navy destroyer to be an all-welded construction. Stationed on home waters in 1953, she was the first naval vessel to be despatched to the aid of the Princess Victoria on 31 January 1953.

Born in 1922, 'Mac' McArdle joined the Navy in 1938 as a boy seaman, 2nd class, and served throughout the Second World War as a torpedoman. He passed a fleet board for promotion to officer while serving in Colombo at the end of the war, and quickly proved his efficacy as an excellent officer. In 1952 as guard officer of the naval barracks at Chatham,

he trained the naval guard for the funeral of King George VI and became a Member of the Royal Victorian Order.

On 31 January 1953 McArdle was a lieutenant commander and second-in-command aboard the destroyer HMS Contest, which was sheltering in Rothesay during some of the worst winter weather on record in Britain. The ship

◄ McArdle as a young naval officer.

picked up a distress signal from the MV *Princess Victoria*, a car ferry in the North Channel en route from Stranraer to Larne.

Built in 1947, the *Princess Victoria* was the first car ferry of it type to operate in British coastal waters. Under the command of Captain James Ferguson, who had sailed the same route for the previous 17 years, the ferry left Stranraer at 0745 hours with 128 passengers and 51 crew. Heavy seas had buckled the stern doors, and despite the crew's efforts, they could not be closed. Water flooded into the car deck and the ferry began listing dangerously. Two hours after leaving Stranraer, the radio operator sent a distress signal: 'Hove-to off mouth of Loch Ryan. Vessel not under command. Urgent assistance of tugs required.' An hour later, with water still flooding in, an SOS call was made and the captain gave the order to abandon ship. A final message was received at 1358 hours, stating that the ship was 'on her beam end'.

HMS *Contest* set out to assist the stricken vessel, but despite arriving at the *Victoria's* last known position at 1330 hours, could not find the ship. *Contest* finally sighted wreckage from the vessel at 1523 hours. The officers and crew

immediately began looking for survivors.

In rough seas, McArdle supervised the rescue operations from the upper deck, hauling people from the sea. In late afternoon, McArdle saw a survivor clinging to a life raft, but, as the sea surged, the man lost his grip. McArdle immediately tied a lifeline around his waist and leapt into the water to help him. He dragged him to the ship's safety nets, but the effort exhausted him. Chief Petty Officer Wilfrid Warren dived in to help both men, and as the destroyer rolled in the sea, all three were dragged under. Somehow, all three men were safely pulled aboard.

Only 44 people survived the wreck of the *Princess Victoria*, all of them men. The women and children had been dispatched in a lifeboat that was smashed against the side of the ferry, with no survivors. The disaster shocked the British public, not least because it occurred on what was regarded as a short, safe crossing.

Selfless and courageous, McArdle and Warren were both awarded the George Medal for their 'gallantry and presence of mind'. McArdle went on to a distinguished naval career, achieving the rank of rear admiral before his retirement in 1982.

▲ HMS Burghead, *a Bay-class anti-aircraft frigate, was McArdle's first command in 1957 on the South Atlantic Station. McArdle was later commended as a 'most efficient commanding officer who has run a well-organised and happy ship'.*

RIFLEMAN DEBILAL RANA

MM

awarded 25 October 1955 • Malaya • 1st/2nd Gurkha Rifles

▼ The MM was established in 1916 as the other ranks' equivalent of the MC. It was awarded throughout the 20th century until 1993, when the MC became available to all ranks.

Rifleman Debilal Rana epitomised the qualities for which the Gurkhas have become renowned, displaying tenacity, courage and a cold-blooded efficiency in combat. Rifleman Debilal fought throughout the Malayan Emergency and, as his citation said, 'distinguished himself by his bravery, coolness under fire and determination to come to grips with the enemy'.

In the wake of the Second World War and the subsequent independence of India, the Gurkha regiments were split between the British army and the newly formed independent Indian army. The 2nd Gurkha Rifles was one of four regiments transferred to the British. Malaya, like other areas of the shrinking British Empire, had its own share of troubles, as insurgents tried to ensure not only an independent future for Malaya, but one in which Communist rule would be assured. The British naturally wished to exert control over any independence process and recognised that, in both practical and ideological terms, a Communist regime in Malaya was not in Britain's best interests.

The insurgency campaign was one of terror, characterised by vicious attacks against European and native inhabitants,

interspersed with jungle warfare. The Communists used a combination of tactics to win the hearts and minds of local people – either bribery or terrifying coercion. The British used more effective long-term tactics to win over the native people, and responded to the Communist threat with aggression. Despite their efforts, the 'Emergency' continued for 12 years, and the Gurkha regiments formed the backbone of the British military response. (It was called an 'Emergency' because, had it been called a 'war', losses would not have been covered by insurance.)

The Gurkha regiments were ideally equipped to deal with the guerrilla tactics of the Communist cells. Many of the soldiers had fought in the Far East during the Second World War and were familiar with the type of terrain and the nature of jungle warfare.

Rifleman Debilal Rana was based at Kota Tinggi, the site of the Commonwealth jungle warfare school. He was a member of the 1st/2nd Gurkha Rifles, whose work, like that of many other units,

> In a regiment of extraordinary fighters, Debilal demonstrated exceptional bravery that saw him awarded the Military Medal.

consisted of patrolling the jungle, protecting the new villages and denying the Communists access to their supplies and bases. It was tense, relentless soldiering that required constant alertness, and swift and decisive reactions.

A highly experienced Gurkha, Rifleman Debilal Rana consistently demonstrated dedication to the cause: he personally accounted for the deaths of three terrorists and fought in many more actions that resulted in the capture or death of dozens more Communist insurgents. In a regiment of extraordinary fighters, Debilal demonstrated exceptional bravery that saw him awarded the Military Medal.

In September 1954, his patrol encountered a Communist cell and, having killed two of

them, faced debilitating fire from the third man who was armed with a Sten gun. With no thought for his own protection, Rifleman Debilal very calmly shot him through the head with one shot, even though this action exposed him to mortal danger.

Just three months later, Rifleman Debilal charged a wounded terrorist who had just withdrawn the pin from a grenade and was about to throw it into the middle of his patrol. In the graphic words of the citation, 'The grenade exploded in the terrorist's hand, blowing him to pieces. It was a miracle that Rifleman Debilal himself was unscathed… [and] saved the lives of the other two men in his small patrol'.

▲ *A Gurkha leads a Malay prisoner from a Wessex helicopter.*

PRIVATE HORACE 'SLIM' MADDEN GC

awarded 27 December 1955 • Korea • Royal Australian Regiment

Private Horace 'Slim' Madden's brave and selfless actions earned him the highest decoration to be awarded to an Australian soldier during the Korean War. Captured by the Chinese, he was repeatedly maltreated and yet refused to co-operate in any way with his captors. Furthermore, he shared his meagre rations with his fellow prisoners when he knew that doing so would probably hasten his own demise.

▼ *A pack of North Korean cigarettes given to British POWs during the Korean War.*

Born in 1924, Private Horace 'Slim' Madden was brought up in Sydney, and was mobilised in 1942. He served in New Guinea with the 8th Field Ambulance and on Bouganville with the 5th Motor Ambulance Convoy Platoon. Before his discharge in June 1947, he also served in Japan as part of the British Commonwealth Occupation Force. In August 1950, after working as a nurse for three years, he re-enlisted with the Australian Army, joining the 3rd Battalion Royal Australian Regiment (3 RAR).

3 RAR was the first Australian force to be committed to the Korean War as part of the United Nation's defence of South Korea against the Chinese-Communist-backed forces of North Korea.

The Australians underwent a period of intensive training in Japan before their arrival in Korea in September 1950. Madden arrived in November and served as a linesman in the signals platoon, working in sub-zero temperatures to keep the lines of communication open. On 22 April 1951, 3 RAR was part of the UN force that was supporting South Korean positions at the northern end of the Kapyong Valley. The Australians, together with the Canadian 2nd Battalion Princess Patricia's Canadian Light Infantry, were holding forward positions on behalf of the 27th British Commonwealth Brigade, and they bore the brunt of an immense Chinese attack. The battle of Kapyong was intensely fierce and, as the Australians made a tactical withdrawal in the early hours of 23 April, Private Madden was captured.

Madden and his colleagues Corporal Bob Parker and Private Keith Gwyther were forced to spend the next few days recovering wounded Chinese soldiers from the front, before being marched to 'Bean Camp', a notorious prisoner of war camp. Madden distinguished himself by being relentlessly cheerful, defiant, and refusing to co-operate with the Chinese, who beat him repeatedly. Not surprisingly, his health declined because the prisoners' food rations were poor, and Madden's behaviour meant that he was punished by being deprived of food. Madden willingly gave away the small amount he had to men weaker than himself. He undoubtedly suffered from malnutrition and his condition declined still further in October, when he was among the sick and wounded prisoners forcibly moved 140 miles (225km) to another POW camp at Pingchong-Ni.

Madden died from malnutrition in November/December 1951, having sacrificed his life for his comrades. After the end of hostilities in Korea, many men came forward to commend Madden's inspirational and morale-boosting behaviour. 'Slim was a real hero – and didn't know it,' said Keith Gwyther. 'He became a sort of legend. He didn't try to be like that – it was just the way he was made. Nothing could make him co-operate with the enemy'. His reputation grew and he was posthumously awarded the George Cross in 1955, the highest award given to any Australian soldier in the Korean War.

▲ A portrait of an Australian hero, Private Horace Madden GC, 3rd Battalion Royal Australian Regiment.

◄ A former British POW is given an issue of cigarettes and magazines by the British Red Cross following his release from North Korean captivity in 1953.

HMS Eagle leads HMS Bulwark and HMS Albion, three of the five British aircraft carriers involved in the Suez operation in October 1956. The nationalisation of the Suez Canal by Egypt's President Nasser in 1956 led to armed intervention by British, French and Israeli forces.

WING COMMANDER FREDERICK 'TAFFY' HIGGINSON

OBE, DFC, DFM

awarded (DFM) 27 July 1940 • Battle of Britain • RAF

▼ A flight of Hawker Hurricane Mark I planes of No. 56 Squadron RAF taking off for a sortie over France from North Weald, Essex, in May 1940. In the foreground, another Hurricane Mark I of the Squadron, P2764 'US-P', stands at its dispersal point near the perimeter track on the south-western edge of the airfield.

Wing Commander Frederick 'Taffy' Higginson was a fighter ace during the Second World War, whose experiences are the stuff of movies. One of only 12 pilots to be credited with more than 12 enemy kills, he was shot down over France in June 1941 and eventually made it home 15 months later, helped by the Resistance.

Born in Swansea in 1913, Higginson was a career airman who joined the RAF aged 16 in 1929 as an apprentice fitter and gunner, before training as a pilot in 1935. In 1937 he joined No. 56 Squadron to fly Hawker Hurricanes – then the finest fighter plane in the RAF. By the time war broke out, Higginson was a flight sergeant with ten years' experience under his belt.

In May 1940 his squadron was sent to France to provide air cover for the Dunkirk evacuation, and then to fight throughout the Battle of Britain from their base in the south of England. Sergeant Higginson was sent to France with B Flight, where he shot down four Luftwaffe aircraft, notching up his fifth in the early days of the Battle of Britain and officially becoming an ace in July 1940. He was awarded the Distinguished Flying Medal for 'his cool and courageous leadership'.

Between July and September 1940 he accounted for at least nine more enemy aircraft,

and, despite damage to his Hurricane, and a crash landing, he somehow avoided personal injury. Higginson was commissioned as a pilot officer in September 1940 and promoted in April 1941 to flying officer.

He was finally shot down on 17 June 1941 over Lille in northern France, but he was uninjured and avoided capture by the Germans. He managed to make contact with the local resistance unit and over the following 15 months, Higginson travelled across France, anxious to get home and rejoin his unit. However, having got as far south as Perpignan, he was stopped by gendarmes who discovered that he had false papers. He might have talked his way out, but Higginson hit one of them and was imprisoned for six months. His incarceration was extended still further in March 1942 as a reprisal following an Allied air raid on a local Renault factory.

By this point, the British intelligence services urged their underground contacts to retrieve

Higginson, given his exceptional skills as a pilot. So, on 6 August 1942, Higginson and four other pilots were eased out of their Monte Carlo jail. Accompanied by Father Myrda, a Polish priest, and disguised as priests themselves, Higginson and his comrades were picked up by a Polish fishing trawler from a beach near Perpignan and transferred to the Special Operations Executive fast patrol boat HMS *Minna,* which transported them to Gibraltar. From there, Higginson was flown home to RAF Greenock.

Higginson rejoined No. 56 Squadron – now flying Hawker typhoons – and 'continued to display great skill and courage in combat with the enemy', according to the citation on his Distinguished Flying Cross in 1943. He continued to serve with the RAF until his retirement in 1956, when he began working for British Aerospace in the guided weapons division. In 1969 Higginson retired to a farm in Carmarthanshire and died in 2003 after a long and eventful life.

▲ *A Hawker Typhoon Mark IB of No. 56 Squadron RAF runs up its engine in a revetment at Matlask, Norfolk, before taking off on a 'Rhubarb' (a harassing fighter operation) over Holland. Typhoons were outstanding ground attack aircraft, with powerful engines that allowed them to carry a substantial payload of bombs.*

FLIGHT LIEUTENANT LEONARD GEORGE CALVERT
MC

awarded 1958 • Aden • RAF

Fighting in one of Britain's small and almost undeclared wars, Flight Lieutenant George Calvert was awarded the Military Cross while serving with No. 10 Squadron, Aden Protectorate Levies, on 12 January 1957.

▼ *An armoured car of the Aden Protectorate Levies.*

Aden was a crucial part of Britain's empire; its geographical position on the southern tip of the Arabian peninsula meant that it guarded the entrance to the Red Sea, and therefore the route to the Suez Canal, which, in the days before air power, was the lifeline of the empire. It was a coaling station, and, by the late 1950s, Aden was the busiest port in the world (apart from New York). In the post-war years, the RAF base at Khormaksar was a vital refuelling point for aircraft en route from Europe to the Far East.

The Aden Protectorate Levies (APL) were formed from local troops equipped, trained and led by the British, and were initially intended to defend RAF stations in the Arabian peninsula. In the 1950s, the APL was tasked with safeguarding the Aden Protectorate against incursions from neighbouring Yemen, and with supporting

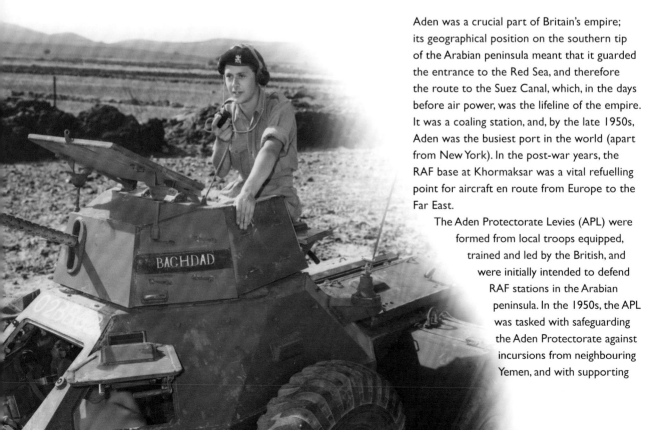

local tribal rulers against local instability. After the Suez crisis of 1956, with Communist-backed skirmishes becoming more frequent, the APL established bases along the Yemeni border. The British were keen that the local rulers should unite to face off the threat from Yemen, but they seemed surprised by the surge of Arab nationalism in the colony after 1956.

Flight Lieutenant Calvert was promoted from the ranks of the RAF Regiment and was commissioned as a pilot officer in 1948. In 1951 he was awarded a short service commission of six years as a flying officer. Calvert served in No. 10 Armoured Car Squadron from 1955 to 1957, commanding Ferret armoured cars, and was based at RAF Khormaksar, the main airfield in Aden (and now the site of Aden International airport).

Calvert's action was one of the last undertaken while the RAF were still in nominal control of the defence of Aden. The regiment was under-resourced and over-stretched, and the decision was taken to let the Army take over responsibility for the area. To give an idea of the intensity of the skirmishes endured, the regiment was awarded one Distinguished Service Cross, seven Military Crosses, two Military Medals, one OBE, three MBEs and one BEM in a single two-year period.

Officers and NCOs of the RAF regiment led local troops on daily patrols into the harsh hinterland of the Aden colony. Their Ferrets were tough vehicles, but the APL faced a determined and well-armed enemy. On 12 January 1957 Calvert's section was on reconnaissance when it came under heavy fire from a Yemeni fort. Instead of retreating, Calvert moved his troop nearer to the fort and engaged the enemy with accurate and sustained fire. His own vehicle was hit over 50 times and the windscreen smashed, yet despite this, Calvert repeatedly fired on the fort, allowing other members of the section to withdraw. His citation reads: 'During this and other operations between 12th and 23rd January 1957, Flight Lieutenant Calvert showed qualities of leadership and command of the highest standard. His complete disregard of his own safety and his example were

During this and other operations between 12th and 23rd January 1957, Flight Lieutenant Calvert showed qualities of leadership and command of the highest standard. His complete disregard of his own safety and his example were the main factors contributing to the magnificent work of 'A' Flight during those operations.

the main factors contributing to the magnificent work of 'A' Flight during those operations.'

Calvert's courage, determination and leadership during what was officially a small colonial skirmish were rightly recognised, and his MC was gazetted 18 months later, in August 1958.

▼ Suk, or market place, Mukeiras. This town, on the border with Yemen, was the centre of much fighting.

COMMANDER HENRY RITCHIE VC

awarded 10 April 1915 • Dar es Salaam • Royal Navy

Henry Ritchie was the first member of the Royal Navy to be awarded the Victoria Cross during the First World War, for his leadership of a raiding party during an operation on Dar es Salaam, the capital of the German colony of German East Africa.

▼ *Wreck of the German cruiser* Konigsberg *in the Rufiji River Delta in 1916. The Konigsberg was finally sunk in July 1915 having been bombarded by British monitors and scuttled by her crew.*

Ritchie was born and raised in Edinburgh before joining the Royal Navy and entering the training ship HMS *Britannia* at the age of 14 in 1890. At the outbreak of the First World War he was a commander on the pre-Dreadnought battleship

HMS *Goliath*, which was sent to blockade the German port of Dar es Salaam on the east coast of Africa. The Admiralty was concerned that the port could prove useful as a base for German commerce raiders operating in the Indian Ocean, and indeed the SMS *Konigsberg* had operated from Dar es Salaam before taking refuge in the Rufiji River Delta to the south of Dar es Salaam in September, where she was blockaded by warships of the Royal Navy.

A number of German merchant ships remained in Dar es Salaam's harbour and it was decided to neutralise them to prevent their supplying any other German commerce raiders. The Germans had blocked the entrance to the harbour to prevent the British capital ships getting through, so volunteers were assembled from throughout the squadron and a raiding force assembled that would use small ships to penetrate the harbour. Commander Ritchie was put in command of the expedition.

Having warned the Germans of the raid the day before, in order that they might evacuate the ships to prevent unnecessary loss of life, the raiding party went in on the morning of

28 November and initially met no opposition. Ritchie placed demolition charges on a number of the merchant vessels, before proceeding further down the harbour until his ship became grounded on a sandbar; returning to the merchant ships he discovered empty ammunition boxes and realised that the German seaman meant to ambush his party as it left. Despite this he resolved to carry out his task and as the party made its withdrawal it came under heavy fire from the shore.

Ritchie attempted to pick up some of the men left aboard the German vessels, but this was unsuccessful and as he retreated from the harbour he came under rifle, machine-gun and artillery fire. Most of the men on the boat were wounded, but Ritchie kept to the helm until he had managed to steer the boat back to HMS *Goliath*. He had suffered eight separate wounds in the course of the action, as his citation reveals: 'Though severely wounded several times his fortitude and resolution enabled him to continue to do his duty inspiring all by his example until at his eighth wound he became unconscious.'

The severity of his wounds meant that Ritchie never returned to active service and retired from the Navy in 1917. He passed away in 1958.

▼ The battleship HMS Goliath, from which Henry Ritchie launched his raid on Dar es Salaam. She was torpedoed and sunk off Cape Helles in the Dardanelles on 13 May 1915.

" Though severely wounded several times his fortitude and resolution enabled him to continue to do his duty inspiring all by his example until at his eighth wound he became unconscious. "

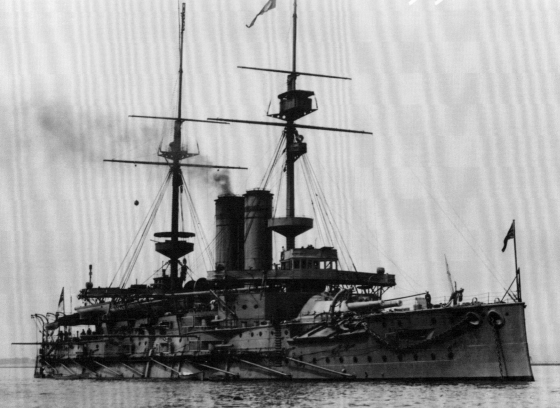

COLONEL SIR HUGH BRASSEY
KCVO, OBE, MC, DL, JP

awarded (MC) 11 October 1945 • Northwest Europe • Royal Scots Greys

Hugh Brassey was a professional soldier who was awarded the Military Cross and the Croix de Guerre for his courage and leadership during the Normandy campaign in 1944. He went on to serve as commander of the Royal Wiltshire Yeomanry and was awarded the OBE in 1959.

▼ *A Stuart tank of the Royal Scots Greys, 4th Armoured Brigade in Wismar, 4 May 1945.*

Brassey was born in 1915 and educated at Eton College and Sandhurst. He was commissioned into the Royal Scots Greys in 1935. One of the great cavalry regiments of the British Army, the Royal Scots Greys was still largely mounted on horses in the inter-war years, and it was not until 1940 that the regiment became fully mechanised. Brassey fought in the Syria-Lebanon campaign of 1941, where he was machine-gun officer during the hard-fought campaign against the Vichy French in Syria. In 1942 the regiment became part of the 8th Army and was transferred to Egypt. Brassey commanded A Squadron of the Scots Greys at Alamein, where it was reported that the Scots Greys used their tanks almost as if they were still mounted on horses, by charging German artillery at Fuka and capturing 11 artillery pieces.

Brassey moved on to command C Squadron in Tripoli as the regiment prepared to take part in the invasion of Italy. In 1943 the Royal Scots Greys were re-equipped with Sherman tanks and, as commander of D Squadron, Brassey took part in the Salerno landings in September 1943, fighting German forces in the advance to Naples. The regiment continued to advance north until stopped at the Gargiliano River, which was at the centre of the defensive lines around Monte Cassino.

Brassey was transferred back to England to command HQ Squadron, while the regiment was trained and re-fitted in preparation for the Normandy Invasions. The tanks of the Royal Scots Greys landed on Juno beach on D Day+1. Brassey led B Squadron across north-west Europe, leading the regiment's Sherman tanks as they struggled against the superior Panther tanks of the German armoured divisions in the breakout from Normandy. By now a major, Brassey demonstrated courage and leadership that earned him an MC and, rather more unusually, the Croix de Guerre, awarded by a grateful French nation to those who worked so hard to liberate their country.

After the war, Brassey moved to command the Royal Wiltshire Yeomanry from 1955 until 1958. His leadership while the regiment converted from heavy armour to a light reconnaissance role proved critical, and he was appointed OBE in 1959.

Brassey enjoyed the kind of traditional, yet highly valuable, career typical of many men of his age and class, serving his country in both war and peace. He became High Sheriff of Wiltshire in 1959 and an officer of the Yeoman of the Guard, the Queen's ceremonial bodyguard, in 1964. He was Lord Lieutenant of Wiltshire from 1981 to 1989 (having been both Deputy Lord Lieutenant and Vice Lord Lieutenant since 1956). For his many years of pubic service, Brassey was invested as a Knight of the Royal Victorian Order on his retirement in 1985, an award within the personal gift of the monarch.

WARRANT OFFICER MICK FLYNN
CGC, MC

awarded (CGC) 31 October 2003 • Iraq and Afghanistan • Blues and Royals

Warrant Officer Mick Flynn, a veteran of campaigns in Northern Ireland, the Falklands, Iraq, Bosnia and Afghanistan, is Britain's most highly decorated frontline soldier. He has experienced some of the fiercest fighting of the last 30 years and has received two of Britain's highest awards for bravery, the Conspicuous Gallantry Cross and the Military Cross.

▼ Corporal Major of Horse Mick Flynn with armoured vehicles of the Blues and Royals Regiment in the Windsor barracks.

Born in Cardiff in 1960, Mick Flynn joined the army at the age of 16 and was assigned to the Blues and Royals. He saw service in Northern Ireland, where, aged only 18, he witnessed the death of a colleague at close quarters on the Falls Road. Battle-hardened, he served in the Falklands, where he took part in the operation to capture Mount Tumbledown.

Flynn left the army in 1993 after 15 years' service, but re-joined less than ten years later at the age of 41 at a lower rank. After re-training, he was posted to Iraq, where in 2003 he earned the CGC, Britain's second-highest medal for bravery. His reconnaissance vehicle discovered the entire Iraqi 4th Armoured Division almost by chance, and as he radioed this news to the command post, Flynn's vehicle called down more artillery fire than any other in the war. During this action he also succeeded in holding enemy tanks at bay while wounded men were evacuated from vehicles hit by US A-10 'friendly fire'. Commanding a Scimitar. Flynn played a deadly game of cat and mouse with the Iraqi armour for seven days. He was outgunned and outnumbered, but fired on some and directed attacks on others with, as his citation said, 'no consideration for his own safety'.

Three years later, Flynn distinguished himself again, this time during his first operational tour in Helmand Province, Afghanistan. His Scimitar tank was leading a column of four armoured vehicles through an Afghan village, when it was ambushed and hit by rocket-propelled grenades and heavy machine-gun fire, which disabled but did not destroy the vehicle. The Spartan Armoured Personnel Carrier behind was engulfed in flames,

and although it looked as though no one could have survived the blast, Flynn decided to go back into the ambush to find his comrades. Flynn provided covering fire against some 30 Taliban fighters, while two of his crew pulled what appeared to be the charred remains of Trooper Martyn Compton to safety. Compton suffered 70 per cent burns, but he survived the incident thanks to the courage and gallantry of Flynn and his colleagues. Flynn's unthinking bravery earned him the MC.

Despite the fact that he has seen action in all of Britain's major military engagements since 1979, Flynn has fortunately never been badly injured in battle. He sustained his most serious wound in a nightclub stabbing in Paphos.

Flynn's reputation within the British Army is the stuff of legend, partly because of his length of service (albeit interrupted). He is one of the oldest NCOs in the army, but his very experience, his bravery, and his ability to remain calm under pressure mean that he has earned the respect of every man with whom he serves.

▲ Troops of the 3rd Battalion the Parachute Regiment were supported by Flynn's unit, D Squadron Household Cavalry, as they carried out an operation in the Taliban stronghold town of Nowzad, Helmand Province, Afghanistan in 2006.

▼ Scimitar tanks of D Squadron Household Cavalry leaving camp in Kuwait, 2003.

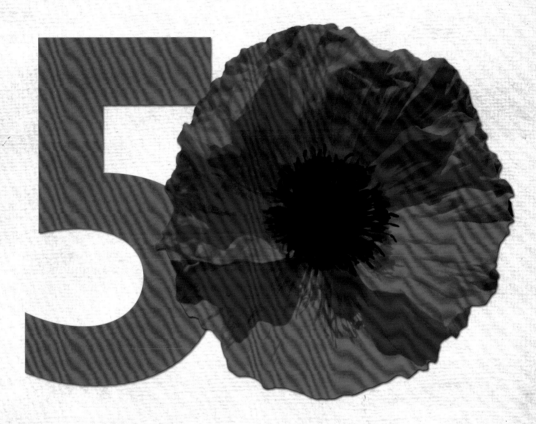

CHAPTER FIVE

1961–1970 **Change and renewal**

▼ *The need for renewal and modernisation was clear, and attempts were made to update the Poppy Appeal for a new generation.*

The 1960s saw a changing of the guard in the Legion, as the original founders and those who had driven it through its early days began to pass away. Sir Frederick Lister, who had served as the first chairman and done so much to bring together the disparate ex-service organisations into one unified force, died in 1966. And 1970 saw General Sir Charles Jones take on the role of Legion president, the first man to occupy this post who had not served in the First World War. The presidents over the decade – General Sir Richard Howard-Vyse and General Sir Oliver Leese – were very much in the mould of Earl Haig, reflecting the first president's belief that those who had held high rank in the armed forces had a duty of care to those they led. However, the 1960s saw the reputation of Haig and the other senior commanders of the First World War come under increasing threat. The publication of Alan Clark's *The Donkeys* in 1961 was one of the first shots in this campaign, placing much of the blame for the high casualties in the First World War on the heads of the senior commanders. Then the musical, and subsequent film, *Oh What a Lovely War!*, which debuted in 1963, further demonised Haig, and the Legion was called upon

to defend its first president's reputation. This was a trend throughout the decade, with the rise of the Campaign for Nuclear Disarmament (CND) leading to conflict with the Legion as it sought to hold ceremonies and meetings at war memorials, something that the Legion contested vigorously. The anti-war attitude of the times led to ill-founded accusations that the Legion, Remembrance and even the Poppy Appeal itself all in some way fostered militarism.

The Legion did much to counter these views by embarking on an ambitious public relations drive. This was not only to correct unwanted assumptions, but also to highlight the real and valuable work that the Legion carried out with regard to the welfare of ex-servicemen; to highlight the value of the Legion to those who had finished their National Service; and to emphasise the need for the general public to fully support the Poppy Appeal in what were difficult economic times and when many other charities were all actively seeking public support.

Although there was a great deal of focus on attracting new members and youth into the Legion, the old members were not forgotten. Many veterans of the First World War were now in their seventies, with some of those

1961 — 40th anniversary celebration of the founding of the Legion

1962

1963

1964 — Launch of the British Legion Housing Association

1965 — Death of Sir Winston Churchill

◀ *The lifeboat funded by Legion voluntary contributions as part of the 1971 Jubilee celebrations. The new 'Royal' prefix appears clearly on the bow.*

▼ *Winston Churchill, shown here on his 80th birthday, being presented by an illuminated address by officers of the Legion. Churchill was a staunch supporter, and the Legion took an active role in his funeral procession in 1965.*

of the Second World War approaching their sixties. Many of their problems involved accommodation, and one of the Legion's greatest achievements of the decade was in setting up the British Legion Housing Association in 1964. This group found the sites for development and managed the properties, while the rents for those living in them were provided by local authority benefits. The first of these developments opened in 1967, and by 1970 six more schemes had been completed, and a further 21 were in development.

1966	1967	1968	1969	1970

Death of Sir Frederick Lister, the first Legion chairman

First broadcast of the Festival of Remembrance in colour

SIMON WESTON
OBE

awarded 1992 • charity fundraising • Welsh Guards

For those who grew up in the wake of the Second World War – children born in the 1960s – Simon Weston was the first dreadful and yet inspiring example of true heroism of their own generation. Horribly wounded in the Falklands War, Simon Weston faced his future with courage, and has used his experiences to help others.

Born in Caerphilly in 1961, Weston joined the Welsh Guards aged 16, and saw service in Berlin, Northern Ireland and Kenya. In 1982, Britain declared war on Argentina, which had annexed the Falklands Islands in the South Atlantic. Prime Minister Margaret Thatcher dispatched a naval task force to travel 8000 miles (12 870km) with the intention of liberating the islands via an ambitious amphibious assault. The Welsh Guards sailed south on 12 May aboard the RMS *Queen Elizabeth II*, and on 8 June 1982 they were aboard the landing ship HMS *Sir Galahad*, preparing to land at Fitzroy Cove on East Falkland, when the ship was attacked by Argentine fighter planes. *Sir Galahad*, which was carrying fuel and ammunition, caught fire.

The Welsh Guards suffered terrible loss of life, with over 22 men in Weston's 30-man platoon dying in the fierce blaze. Weston himself survived, but suffered 46 per cent burns. Not only was he barely recognisable, but he underwent years of reconstructive surgery and endured the psychological trauma of post-traumatic stress. He has admitted that he resorted to drink and felt suicidal on occasion, but he somehow overcame these feelings and has managed to use his experiences to help others.

What is remarkable is that Weston had the mental fortitude to overcome his own problems, which is a great achievement in itself. That he has been able to reach out to others and become an inspiring motivational speaker, as well as the public face of a number of charities, is even more laudable. As he has said himself, his war injuries have, in many ways, been the making of him.

In 1986 the Guards Association asked him to tour Australia to raise awareness of the plight of burns victims. For the first time since his accident Weston began to feel truly useful, as he saw donations to children's burns units rise as a direct result of his visit. Weston is now the patron of a number of charities that support people with disfigurement, and he was awarded an OBE in 1992 for his tireless charity work.

▼ *Simon Weston, photographed at the Cheltenham Literature Festival, October 2008.*

Simon Weston has a successful career as a motivational speaker, putting his own experiences to good use in an attempt to encourage others to embrace whatever challenges life throws up. With three autobiographies under his belt and a strong media presence, Simon Weston has helped to ensure that public perception of the needs of ex-soldiers and the victims of accidents remain strong. He has worked with victims of the 2005 bombings in London and supports the Royal Star and Garter Homes, which provide nursing and therapeutic support for ex-service personnel. He has spoken out against the military intervention in Iraq, and has added his voice to the debate about the military covenant.

In short, Simon Weston has spent his life since 1982 using his extraordinary experiences to encourage others and inspire them not to give up in the face of seemingly insurmountable problems.

▲ *The burning hulk of HMS* Sir Galahad *in Fitzroy Cove, 8 June 1982. A total of 50 men were killed and many more wounded when* Sir Galahad *was attacked by five Argentinian A4 Skyhawks.*

▼ *The crest of the Welsh Guards laid out on a memorial in the Falkland Islands by relatives of those who died in the conflict.*

COMMANDER NIGEL 'SHARKEY' WARD

DSC, AFC

awarded (DSC) 11 October 1982 • Falklands War • Fleet Air Arm

▼ A formation of Royal Navy FRS.1 Sea Harriers, each representing one of the three Naval Air Squadrons that took part in the Falklands War. Naturally they include a Harrier from Ward's own No. 801 Naval Air Squadron.

As the senior Sea Harrier pilot in the Royal Navy Task Force that was sent from Great Britain to reclaim the Falkland Islands, Lieutenant Commander Ward advised the Task Force commander on air warfare strategy and tactics. He also flew more than 60 missions over the islands, and shot down three Argentinian aircraft. He was duly awarded the Distinguished Service Cross for his gallantry.

Nigel 'Sharkey' Ward joined the Royal Navy in 1962, and trained as a pilot in the Fleet Air Arm. Although he flew several different types of aircraft, he was most closely associated with the Sea Harrier, which first entered service with the Royal Navy in 1980. When the Argentinians invaded the Falkland Islands in 1982, a naval Task Force was assembled to help recapture the British Overseas Territory. Ward was tasked with assembling the force of Sea Harriers that would provide air cover for the Task Force, and support ground operations. When the Task Force sailed, twenty of the versatile jets were embarked, the force divided between the two carriers: HMS *Hermes* and HMS *Invincible*.

As the commander of No. 801 Naval Air Squadron based on the light aircraft carrier HMS *Invincible*, and as the senior Sea Harrier pilot embarked in the deployment, Lieutenant Commander Ward advised the Task Force commander, Rear Admiral Woodward, on the strategy and tactics of air warfare. He therefore played a significant role in shaping the course of Britain's successful campaign.

As well as advising the admiral, 'Sharkey' Ward led his squadron in action by planning missions, and taking part in air operations when the Task Force came within range of the enemy-occupied islands. As the leading night-flying pilot in the Task Force, Ward made good use of his experience during the campaign, flying numerous night patrols and missions from his carrier.

He was a highly respected and inspirational leader, who cared for his pilots, and sought to minimise the risk to them, while making the best possible use of their expertise, and the versatility of their aircraft.

He was also at the forefront of the fighting; on 1 May he engaged a flight of three T-34C Turbo-Mentors that were attacking a Royal Navy Sea King helicopter, damaging one and driving the rest off. Then, on 21 May, he used his 30mm canons to shoot down an Argentinian Pucara. Later that day, Ward and his wingman Lieutenant Steve Thomas engaged three Mirage Vs, all of which were shot down. Thomas claimed two kills and Ward one, all the hits achieved using Sidewinder missiles. Ward scored his third kill on 1 June, when he shot down a C-130 Hercules transport plane about 60 miles (96km) north of the Falklands, using his cannons. Unlike his previous victories, this kill claimed the lives of the aircraft's crew. It is little wonder that the press and his colleagues dubbed him 'Mister Sea Harrier'.

▲ *Lieutenant Commander Nigel 'Sharkey' Ward, AFC, RN, Commanding Officer of No. 801 Naval Air Squadron, Fleet Air Arm, on board HMS* Invincible.

▼ *FRS.1 Sea Harriers of No. 801 Squadron hovering over HMS* Invincible *during the Falklands conflict.*

BRIGADIER HELEN S. CATTANACH
CB, RRC

awarded (RRC) 1963 • British Army Nursing Service

As the Director of British Army Nursing Services, and a brigadier, Helen Cattanach held the most senior rank available to a woman in the British Army. During over half a century of service she transformed the role of military nursing in the British Army.

▼ A nurse of the Queen Alexandra's Imperial Military Nursing Service, pictured in full uniform, treats a patient in a British Army military hospital, during the Second World War, *by Robert Austin RA.*

Helen Cattanach was born in 1920 in the small Highland village of Knockando in Moray, and throughout her long and distinguished medical career she never lost sight of her rural Scottish roots. She was educated in nearby Elgin Academy, and, on leaving school shortly before the outbreak of the Second World War, she chose to follow a career in nursing. She received her training in Woodend Hospital in Aberdeen, and finally became a state registered nurse in the middle of the conflict.

Feeling she had to use her newly acquired skills in the service of her country, she enrolled in the Civil Nursing Reserve (CNR), which was formed by the Ministry of Health at the start of the war to provide nursing staff to deal with the high number of civilian casualties expected from enemy air raids. She served in the CNR until after the end of the war.

In 1946 Helen became a Nursing Sister in the Queen Alexandra's Imperial Military Nursing Service (QAIMNS), the nursing branch of the British Army, and administered by Army Medical Services. She established herself as one of the Service's most gifted nursing sisters, and served

Then, in 1968, she became the Matron at the British military hospital in Münster in West Germany, and the following year she took on the same role in Aldershot in Hampshire, at the largest military hospital in the British Army. Helen's efforts there were rewarded in 1972 when she was promoted to the rank of Brigadier, and made the Matron-in-Chief and Director of the Army's Nursing Services – QARANC. She held this post until 1977, when she retired, after more than three decades of service to military nursing. She died in 1994.

◀ *Brigadier Helen S. Cattanach, CB, RRC.*

▼ *A wartime poster advertising the important work of the Civil Nursing Reserve. The nurses of this organisation made their greatest contribution during the Blitz, and during subsequent air attacks on British cities.*

in a variety of army medical establishments, both at home and abroad. In 1949 the Service was renamed Queen Alexandra's Royal Army Nursing Corps (QARANC), by which time Helen had demonstrated a gift as a nursing administrator.

In 1958, Helen's skills were properly recognised when she was appointed as a Staff Officer of the British Army Medical Directorate (AMD) based in Andover in Hampshire, although she served in the War Office in London's Whitehall, advising her superiors on nursing matters within the British Army. She was therefore able to influence the development of her profession within the service. Three years later, in 1961, she became the first officer in the QARANC to serve in the recruiting arm of the AMD, doing her utmost to recruit others into the job she loved. However, afterwards she elected to return to active nursing, and became a Ward Sister in a British military hospital in Hong Kong that dealt with soldiers injured in the Borneo Confrontation. In 1963 Major Cattanach was awarded the Royal Red Cross for her exceptional service to military nursing.

BANNISTER

CIVIL NURSING RESERVE

WOMEN WANTED

AS NURSING AUXILIARIES

NA

APPLY TO THE CENTRAL EMERGENCY COMMITTEE FOR NURSING, ROMNEY HOUSE, MARSHAM STREET, LONDON, S.W.I. OR LOCALLY TO THE MEDICAL OFFICER OF HEALTH FOR THE COUNTY OR COUNTY BOROUGH · THE ORDER OF ST. JOHN, THE BRITISH RED CROSS SOCIETY OR WOMENS VOLUNTARY SERVICES

NATIONAL SERVICE

MAJOR GENERAL IAIN PATRICK CRAWFORD

GM, MRCS

awarded (GM) 18 December 1964 • Borneo Confrontation • RAMC and 1/7th Gurkha Rifles

▼ *A captain in the Royal Army Medical Corps examines a Murut child, whose parents have fled from Indonesian Borneo to Sarawak, July 1965.*

As a doctor in the Royal Army Medical Corps, Patrick Crawford saved the life of a fellow officer following a helicopter crash in the jungle of Borneo, carrying out an emergency operation that earned him the George Medal. He went on to have a distinguished career in military surgery.

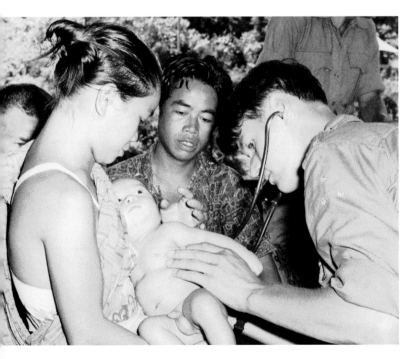

Patrick Crawford (1936–2009) was born in London, the son of a doctor, but was educated at Chatham House Grammar School in Kent. After leaving school he studied medicine at St Thomas' Hospital Medical School in London, and duly qualified as a doctor. He specialised in surgery, and attained membership of the Royal College of Surgeons (MRCS) before becoming a house surgeon at the Royal Sussex County Hospital in 1959. The following year he was called up for National Service, and was commissioned into the Royal Army Medical Corps (RAMC). He was attached to 20th Rgt. Royal Artillery, and then the 1/7th Gurkhas. He saw active service in Malaya before accompanying the battalion to Borneo, where Britain and her Commonwealth allies were engaged in a confrontation with Indonesia, who was using military force to undermine the independence of Malaysia.

On 20 April 1964 Captain Crawford boarded a Wessex helicopter to visit a forward base close to the Sarawak-Indonesian border. He was accompanied by Major 'Birdie' Smith DSO, and six Gurkhas. As the helicopter came in to land its engine failed, and it crashed, tumbling down a steep ravine before becoming impaled on a tree stump. Smith's right arm was crushed during the crash, and he became trapped in the wreckage. Crawford helped the six Gurkhas escape, then examined Smith, who was hanging by his shattered arm. He realised that Smith's only chance of survival was an immediate amputation. So, while supporting Smith's weight for almost an hour, Crawford sawed off the arm using a clasp knife, despite the risk of the helicopter exploding in flames at any moment. There was no morphine, and Smith remained conscious throughout.

Crawford then dressed the wound, and remained to supervise the rescue of his patient by a stretcher party sent from the base. Despite his exhaustion Crawford flew with Smith to the casualty station at Simmanggang and the military hospital in Kuching, and assisted the medical staff in both medical centres until he was assured that Smith would survive his harrowing ordeal. He was subsequently awarded the GM for his actions. Major Smith recovered from his injury, and returned to Borneo the following year to take command of a Gurkha battalion.

Afterwards, Crawford specialised in preventive medicine. From 1968 he spent four years developing military cures for malaria, and serving as a surgical instructor in the military hospital in Singapore. In 1972 he was seconded to the Australian Army, and held a visiting lectureship in surgery at Queensland University. Subsequently, he worked in the Army Medical Directorate, and as the Director of Army Health in the British Army of the Rhine (BAOR). A professorship in the Royal Army Medical College followed, and another secondment, this time to the Saudi Army. He finally retired in 1991.

▼ A helicopter on a jungle airstrip in Borneo. During the Borneo Confrontation helicopters such as this were an essential tool, used to ferry men and equipment to isolated forward bases in the jungle.

CAPTAIN RAMBAHADUR LIMBU
VC, MVO

awarded (VC) 22 April 1966 • Borneo Confrontation • 2/10th Gurkha Rifles

On 21 November 1965, Lance Corporal Limbu took part in Operation Time Keeper, a daring cross-border raid on an Indonesian hilltop base. During the assault Limbu rescued wounded comrades under fire, and then stormed an enemy machine-gun nest. His well-earned decoration was the only Victoria Cross awarded during the Borneo Confrontation.

▼ *Captain Rambahadur Limbu VC, arriving at St. Martin-in-the-Fields in London for a service of remembrance held during a Victoria Cross and George Cross Association reunion.*

Rambahadur Limbu was born in the small village of Chyangthapu in eastern Nepal. Like many boys of the Nepalese Begha clan, he wanted to join the Gurkhas, who served in the British Army. Despite his small stature he was selected, and after initial training he joined the 2nd Battalion of the 10th Gurkha Rifles (Princess Mary's Own). Limbu saw service in Malaya before his regiment was posted to Brunei in December 1962, to assist in the suppression of the Indonesian-backed Brunei Revolt. Limbu saw action against local guerillas, and again in subsequent tours in Borneo by the battalion. The aim of the British was to help defend what had become Eastern Malaysia from Indonesian aggression.

By 1964 it was clear that Indonesian raids could be stopped only by a more aggressive stance, and so Operation Claret was initiated – a series of well-planned and top-secret raids across the Sarawak border into Kalimantan (Indonesian Borneo), to disrupt Indonesian forces there. In November 1965, on its third Borneo tour, C Company of 2/10th Gurkhas were ordered to assault an Indonesian camp, located on top of a hill near the Kalimantan village of Babang.

The attackers were spotted by an Indonesian sentry as they were moving into position, so the Gurkha commander ordered an immediate assault. After capturing the base headquarters, 7 Platoon advanced along the hilltop, covered by Lance Corporal Limbu's light machine gun (LMG) team. The platoon came under heavy machine-gun fire, so he led his team around the flank to a position where they could fire on the enemy.

His two colleagues were wounded, but Limbu managed to carry them both back to safety. Unfortunately, they soon died of their wounds. An enraged Limbu then took the Bren LMG, and firing it from his hip he charged the Indonesian position above him, killing four of the enemy and ending the threat to his platoon. For his great courage he was awarded the VC, the 13th awarded to a Gurkha, and the first to someone of the Limbu clan. His citation (above right) pays tribute to his 'outstanding personal bravery'.

A modest Limbu attributed his survival under fire to his smallness of stature.

Limbu remained with the battalion until he retired in 1985, by which time he had become a Queen's Gurkha Officer with the rank of captain. During his final years in the service he became the Queen's Gurkha Orderly Officer, for which duty he became a Member of the Victorian Order (MVO) in 1984. He now lives in Damak, in his native Nepal.

> " His outstanding personal bravery, selfless conduct, complete contempt of the enemy and determination to save the lives of the men of his fire group set an incomparable example and inspired all who saw him. "

A Wessex helicopter picks up a British Army patrol in Borneo in August 1964.

A patrol from the Queen's Own Highlanders searches the jungles of Brunei for rebels, arms and ammunition during the Brunei Revolt of 1962–63. The Brunei Revolt was part of a series of British military commitments in the Far East during the long retreat from Empire.

GROUP CAPTAIN KENNETH HUBBARD

OBE, DFC, AFC

awarded (DFC) 24 April 1945 • Occupied France • RAF

In 1966, Group Captain Hubbard retired from the RAF after more than a quarter of a century of service. He is best remembered as the pilot of the Valiant bomber that dropped Britain's first live H-Bomb over the Pacific Ocean in 1957.

The son of a professional footballer, Kenneth G. Hubbard (1920–2004) was born in Norwich in Norfolk. He trained as a draughtsman before the outbreak of the Second World War, but in 1940 he decided to become a pilot, and joined the Royal Air Force. He was commissioned in May 1941, and for the next two years he served as a flying

instructor. In late 1943 he was sent to the Middle East to train on the Wellington bomber, before being posted to No. 70 Squadron in Italy, where he flew the Wellington on operational sorties over German-held territory in northern Italy, Romania and Bulgaria. He ended the war as a squadron leader, and was awarded a DFC for his services.

▶ *Three British strategic 'V-Bombers' in flight – a Vickers Valiant similar to the one flown by Hubbard, flanked by an Avro Vulcan and a Handley-Page Victor. These three types of aircraft formed the core of Britain's strategic nuclear bombing force.*

He spent the immediate post-war years on the flying staff of the Empire Armament School in Lincolnshire, and at the RAF Flying School. He made several long-range bomber flights as far as South Africa and Canada during this period, to test the improved performance of fully laden British bombers. In 1954 he assumed command of the RAF station at Shaibah in Iraq, and was awarded the OBE for his services there during the political upheaval that followed the Persian nationalisation of the oil refinery at Abadan. After a Staff College course in 1956, Hubbard became a wing commander, and the commander of No. 40 Squadron, which was equipped with the new Vickers Valiant jet-powered strategic bomber.

Meanwhile British scientists had developed a Hydrogen bomb, which was 70 times more powerful than the atomic bomb dropped over Hiroshima in 1945. They were designed to be dropped from Vickers Valiants, and Hubbard's squadron was duly ordered to take part in Operation Grapple, the testing of these H-Bombs in the central Pacific basin. In May 1957 Hubbard commanded the flight earmarked to undertake the tests. On 15 May he took off from Christmas Island, and, when given the order, he dropped the bomb from a height of 45 000 feet (13 720m). The test was a success, and over the next three weeks Hubbard's crews dropped two more weapons. On his return home, Hubbard was awarded the Air Force Cross.

Further tests followed, despite anti-nuclear protests in Great Britain. Hubbard remained a staunch believer in nuclear deterrence, and proud of the role his squadron played in establishing Britain as a nuclear power. Hubbard became a group captain in 1961, and commanded several more bomber airfields until he retired from the service in 1966. He subsequently moved to Suffolk, became a director of an engineering company, and supported the local Air Training Corps. In 1985 his book *Operation Grapple* was published, in which he defended the creation of Britain's nuclear arsenal. Today, the Vickers Valiant bomber used in Operation Grapple is on display in the Royal Air Force Museum in Hendon, London.

▶ The detonation of Britain's first H-Bomb over Malden Island in the Pacific Ocean on 15 May 1957, after being dropped from Hubbard's Vickers Valiant strategic bomber. The picture was taken from an observation aircraft flying above the natural cloud layer.

GROUP CAPTAIN DENNIS DAVID
CBE, DFC AND BAR AFC

awarded (DFC) 31 May 1940 • Battle of France • RAF

Group Captain Dennis David, who retired from the RAF in 1967, was one of the highest-scoring RAF pilots of the early days of the Second World War, with an impressive 11 victories in May 1940 during the Battle of France. David was awarded the Distinguished Flying Cross and Bar within the space of five days for his achievements.

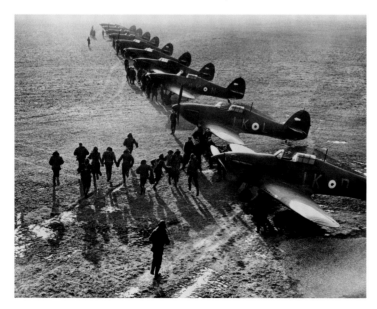

▼ *Pilots of No. 87 Squadron practising a scramble to their Hawker Hurricane Mk I planes at Lille-Seclin, France, in December 1939.*

Dennis David was born in London in 1918 and joined the RAF Volunteer Reserve, starting pilot training in 1937 and obtaining a short service commission the following year. In 1939 he was posted to No. 87 Squadron, which was flying Gloster Gladiators, but soon converted to Hurricanes. In September 1939 this squadron was posted to France as part of the British Expeditionary Force complement on the outbreak of the Second World War. He was involved in one of the rare aerial combats of the Phoney War period, when he damaged a Heinkel III over Poperinghe in November 1939, but his real baptism of fire was to come with the onset of the German Blitzkrieg offensive in May 1940.

On 10 May, the German armies, ably supported by the Luftwaffe, started their advance, and the British forces found themselves overwhelmed, with No. 87 Squadron's base rapidly coming under aerial attack. David, who was on patrol at the time, managed to shoot down one of the attackers and, over the course of the day, he spent some seven hours in the air destroying another German aircraft and damaging a further one. The following day he shot down a Ju 87 and a Do 17, while on the 13th he downed an He III. The ten days he fought in the Battle of France were a constant blur of action and aerial success. However, it could not last, and on 21 May he was shot

▲ Pilots and ground crew gather around the fuselage Balkenkreuz from No. 87 Squadron's first kill, a Heinkel He 111, shot down by Flight Lieutenant Robert Voase-Jeff on 2 November 1939. Pilot Officer Dennis David, who damaged another Heinkel on the same day, autographs the trophy.

down on an early-morning reconnaissance flight, managing to land his badly damaged aircraft. Evacuated back to the UK, the squadron was re-forming in Church Fenton, Yorkshire, when he learnt of the award of his DFC and Bar. The official citation is displayed above right.

Dennis David continued to serve throughout the Battle of Britain with No. 87 Squadron before serving in a wide range of positions for the remainder of the war, finishing his wartime service as a group captain. Remaining in the RAF after the war, he finally retired in 1967. He passed away in 2000.

Since dawn on 10 May 1940, this Officer has shot down four enemy aircraft and shown gallantry and devotion to duty comparable with the highest traditions of the Service. His coolness and determination have been a very fine example to the other Pilots of the Squadron.

▼ A Beaufighter Mark VIF of No. 89 Squadron RAF, running up its engines at Castel Benito, Libya. Dennis David commanded this unit from July 1943 through to March 1944.

LIEUTENANT GEOFFREY HAROLD WOOLLEY
VC, OBE, MC

awarded (VC) 22 May 1915 • Western Front • Queen's Victoria Rifles

▶ *British casualties
of the gas attack on
Hill 60 (near Ypres)
receiving treatment at
No. 8 Casualty Clearing
Station, Bailleul, on
1 May 1915.*

▼ *The Battlefield
of Ypres, by Sir D.Y.
Cameron RA, RSA.
The desolate battlefield
of Ypres, where small
islands of mud surround
flooded bomb craters.*

Lieutenant Woolley, who passed away in 1968, was the first officer of the Territorial Army to be awarded the Victoria Cross in the First World War. He earned his medal in the fierce battle for Hill 60, a crucial position in the Ypres Salient.

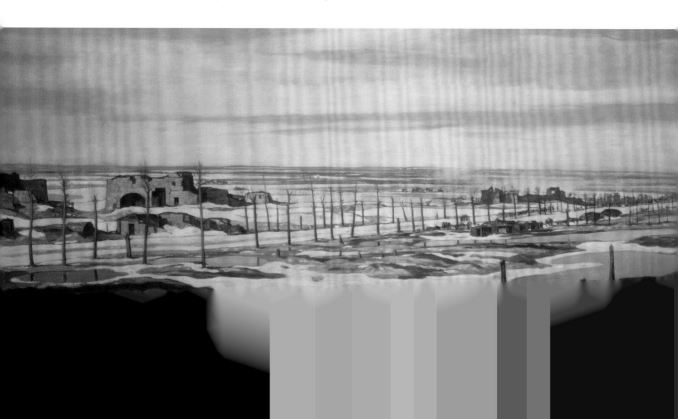

> *Although the only Officer on the hill at the time, and with very few men, he successfully resisted all attacks on his trench, and continued throwing bombs and encouraging his men till relieved. His trench during all this time was being heavily shelled and bombed and was subjected to heavy machine-gun fire by the enemy.*

Geoffrey Woolley was brought up in London and seemed destined for a career in the church until the outbreak of the First World War. He volunteered for duty and was commissioned in the 9th Battalion The London Regiment, popularly known as the Queen Victoria's Rifles. Following training, the battalion was dispatched to France in November 1914 and soon afterwards sent to the Ypres Salient.

Hill 60 was a man-made height that dominated the low-lying ground around Ypres, and had been captured by the Germans in December 1914. It was clear that it had to be retaken and, following a major mining operation, the British recaptured the position on 10 April 1915. It was lost once more to a German counter-attack but regained again on the 18th, with fighting still raging over this hotly contested position.

The Queen Victoria's Rifles were sent up the hill with a resupply of ammunition on the 20th, and were holding the line that night in the face of fierce German attacks. All the other officers on the hill were killed or wounded, leaving Woolley in charge. He refused to withdraw, insisting on remaining at his post until properly relieved. In the face of concerted attacks, Woolley mounted the parapet of the trench and threw grenade after grenade at the advancing

Germans, while the men around him dwindled in number until there were only 20 or so left, out of an original complement of 150.

The position held, and for his courage and leadership Woolley was awarded the VC, with his citation reading: 'Although the only Officer on the hill at the time, and with very few men, he successfully resisted all attacks on his trench, and continued throwing bombs and encouraging his men till relieved. His trench during all this time was being heavily shelled and bombed and was subjected to heavy machine-gun fire by the enemy.'

Hill 60 later fell to the Germans during the Second Battle of Ypres when it was the subject of the first ever poison gas attack. Woolley was appointed as an instructor and served the rest of the war as a staff officer. Following the end of the war he was ordained, later becoming a chaplain in the Army during the Second World War.

WARRANT OFFICER (II) KEITH PAYNE

VC, OAM

awarded 19 September 1969 • Vietnam • AATTV

▼ *An AATTV officer establishes a cordon around a Montagnard village in central South Vietnam before sweeping through to search it.*

Keith Payne was one of the four Australians to be awarded Victoria Crosses for their feats of heroism during the Vietnam War. Payne, despite suffering multiple wounds, led his force of outnumbered local troops against a heavily armed North Vietnamese force.

Keith Payne was born and raised in Queensland, Australia and joined the Australian Army in 1951, serving with the 1st Battalion Royal Australian Regiment in the Korean War. He later served with the 3rd Battalion Royal Australian Regiment in the Malayan Emergency in 1960, as well as in Papua New Guinea in 1967–68, before joining the Australian Army Training Team Vietnam (AATTV) in February 1969. Payne worked with US Special Forces attached to the 1st Mobile Strike Force Battalion, whose 212th Company he commanded. This force was based in the west of the country, reconnoitering NVA (North Vietnamese Army) and Viet Cong infiltration routes from Laos into South Vietnam.

On 24 May, his company was attacked by a superior North Vietnamese force that was equipped with rockets, mortars and machine guns. Payne's men took heavy casualties, and he himself was wounded by shrapnel in the hands, arm and hip while trying to rally them. Deciding to fight his way back to base, Payne regrouped

◀ *Portrait of Warrant Officer Class II, Keith Payne, VC, who was awarded the Victoria Cross for his actions as part of the AATTV. This portrait was painted at Duntroon, Canberra, by Shirley Bourne in 1972.*

▼ *AATTV members get together at the sergeants' mess for the traditional toast after the announcement of Warrant Officer Class II Keith Payne's Victoria Cross. Keith Payne is fourth from the right, while Ray Simpson, to his left, is also a holder of the VC.*

his men and had established a solid defensive perimeter by nightfall. Taking advantage of the cover of darkness, he left this perimeter and crawled out to locate lost and wounded men. Over the course of the next three hours he managed to locate around 40 men, some of whom were wounded, and bring them back to the defensive perimeter. Here he found that the remnants of his company had abandoned the position and retreated to their main base. Undeterred, he led the party of men he had with him back to the battalion base, finally arriving at 0300 hours. For these actions he was recommended for the VC, which was awarded in September 1969 and presented to him by the Queen aboard the Royal Yacht *Britannia* at Brisbane on 13 April 1970. He was also awarded the US Distinguished Service Cross and the South Vietnamese Cross of Gallantry with Bronze Star.

Following his return from Vietnam in September 1969, Payne served as an instructor at the Australian Royal Military College before leaving the army in 1975.

VICE ADMIRAL SIR PETER COMPSTON
KCB

awarded 13 June 1970 • Royal Navy

Sir Peter Compston, had a long and distinguished career in the RAF and the Royal Navy, culminating in his appointment as Deputy Supreme Allied Commander Atlantic in 1968. After his retirement in 1970 he became a highly successful fundraiser for the Royal National Lifeboat Institution (RNLI).

▼ Some of the ship's company of HMS Anson watch the arrival of their new aircraft, a Supermarine Walrus amphibious aircraft. One of the aircraft's crew is sitting on the top wing fixing the Walrus to the crane cable so it can be winched aboard.

Peter Compston was born in 1915. He began his military career by running away from school to enlist in the army as a private soldier, but his family bought him out and, after two years as a stockbroker, he was commissioned into the RAF

in 1936. After he had gained his wings, he joined No. 70 Bomber Squadron in Iraq.

In 1938 Compston transferred to the Fleet Air Arm of the Royal Navy, joining 822 Squadron, which flew Fairey Swordfish torpedo bombers from the aircraft carrier HMS *Furious*. By 1940, he was an experienced pilot, and joined 810 Squadron on HMS *Ark Royal*, bombing German positions in Norway and flying anti-submarine patrols. His career nearly came to an abrupt end during the German invasion of Norway when, with the 1st Battalion Irish Guards, he was aboard the Polish motor ship *Chobry* when it was bombed and sunk by the Luftwaffe.

After a year working as a test pilot on the shore establishment, HMS *Merlin*, Compston assumed command of 700 Squadron's flight of Walrus reconnaissance amphibian planes aboard HMS *Anson* in the North Atlantic in February 1942. Moving to Gibralter in 1943, Compston assisted with the aircraft support logistics in the preparations for the invasion of Italy. His final wartime appointment was at HMS *Flycatcher* in Middle Wallop, where he oversaw the establishment of Mobile Naval Air Bases (MONABs) in the Far East to support the British Pacific Fleet.

In 1945, Compston transferred to a regular naval commission and joined the carrier HMS *Warrior*, serving with the Royal Canadian Navy. He went on to serve in the Korean War as air gunnery officer aboard the light fleet carrier *Theseus* from October 1950 until April 1951. Compston's expertise earned him a Mentioned in Despatches and a promotion.

He achieved his first sea command in 1955 as captain of the destroyer *Orwell*, and, after a period as naval attaché in Paris, he assumed command of the recently modernised carrier HMS *Victorious* in November 1962. He considered this to be the highlight of his career, with *Victorious* carrying the new Buccaneer strike aircraft and tasked with maintaining the security of the newly independent Malayan state.

Promoted to rear admiral in 1965, Compston ended his career with a number of high-profile appointments, as naval attaché in Washington (1965–67) and finally as NATO Deputy Supreme Allied Commander Atlantic in 1970, the same year that he was knighted as KCB.

Compston was more than just a competent officer: he flew more than 30 different types of aircraft during the course of his career and worked hard to ensure that he put his considerable aviation, naval and diplomatic skills to good use in both sea and sky during peace and war. He died on 20 August 2000.

▲ Vice Admiral Sir Peter Compston.

◀ The aircraft carrier HMS Victorious, pictured here in 1959, carried 36 aircraft. When Compston took command, the ship was equipped with Blackburn Buccaneer strike aircraft, which had a nuclear capability.

CHAPTER SIX

1971–1980 Birth of the Royal British Legion

The 1970s was a difficult period for Great Britain in terms of political and social strife. Industrial unrest was particularly marked, with regular confrontations between the unions and the government, which culminated in the miner's strike of 1973 and in the introduction of a three-day week in January 1974. Much of this conflict was caused by rampant inflation, which forced the government of the day to attempt wage caps, while, at the same time, people's wages were struggling to keep up with the cost of everyday goods.

▼ A Metropolitan area parade on London Bridge.

This inflationary curse struck the Legion particularly hard, as not only did its appeals generate less income in real terms, but the increases in cost of living meant that those who were worse off in the ex-service community were ever more in need of their support. The Legion was trapped in a vicious circle. The money generated by the Poppy Appeal was supposed to be kept in reserve, with the interest that was generated being used to support the Legion's day-to-day activities. Instead, the high inflation of the period forced the Legion to divert money directly from the appeal into their benevolent activity, thereby reducing the reserves and further depleting the interest received. Nevertheless the Legion remained steadfast in its devotion to providing for its members' needs.

A boost to the organisation was given with the Legion's jubilee in 1971, which saw its 'Royal' title conferred. There was a great deal of celebration throughout the country and a grand service of re-dedication in Westminster Abbey in May 1971. The Queen's Silver Jubilee in 1977 also saw the Legion rightfully take centre stage in the national celebration, with 2700 standard bearers on parade at Windsor, where the Queen inspected them.

The role of the British Army in Northern Ireland was also coming under increased scrutiny, and was not without its controversies. The first troops had been committed to support the civil power in 1969 and the situation rapidly spiralled out of control. The first British soldier to die in the Troubles was killed in 1971, and the

1971   1972   1973   1974   1975

The Legion's jubilee

(1971–1974) Conflict with the unions sees the introduction of a three-day week

Legion itself was targeted, with the chairman of the Belfast Branch killed in October 1972. Throughout the Troubles, the Legion carried on its work in the community supporting ex-servicemen without any sectarian partisanship, helping to move endangered families out of the province to be re-housed elsewhere in the UK, among other measures. The role of the British Army in Northern Ireland, coupled with the ongoing constant threat of nuclear war – which was amplified by the basing of US cruise missiles in the UK in the early 1980s – meant that the atmosphere was not propitious for the Legion's fundraising activities. However, supported by the jubilee, membership increased slightly in the 1970s and the Legion clubs in particular prospered, with 1060 clubs in existence by 1980, and some 630 000 members out of an overall Legion strength of 740 000.

In other cheering news, the Legion finally claimed victory in their battle for fair war

disability and widow's pensions, with the Government announcing not only a 30 per cent rise in 1974, but also that annual rises thereafter would be linked to the national average wage. With the new Conservative government's removal of tax on these pensions in 1980, the battle was finally won.

1976	1977	1978	1979	1980
	The Queen's Silver Jubilee sees the Legion take an active part		Ceremony of Remembrance at the Cenotaph changed to remember all those who died in the service of their country	Final victory for the Legion in the battle for war pensions

SERGEANT MICHAEL WILLETTS

GC

awarded 20 June 1971 • Northern Ireland • Parachute Regiment

▼ The arrival of British troops on the street of Northern Ireland in 1969 was initially greeted with a degree of relief by the Catholic minority. Relations soon deteriorated, however, and by 1971 violence was a daily occurrence.

Sergeant Michael Willetts was one of the first British soldiers to be killed during the early stages of the Northern Ireland Troubles. A highly experienced soldier, he put himself between a terrorist bomb and civilians, and in doing so, was killed in the ensuing explosion. He was awarded a posthumous George Cross, and is the only para to have been so honoured.

Born in 1943 in Sutton-in-Ashfield, Nottinghamshire, Michael Willetts began his working life underground in the Nottingham coal field. He soon decided that mining was not for him, and enlisted instead in the army, joining the 3rd Battalion, the Parachute Regiment (3 Para) in 1962. He married in October 1965 and had two children. In 1967 he was promoted to corporal and in January 1970 earned his sergeant's stripes. He was a clearly a competent, dedicated and well-respected soldier. His speciality was as a radio operator and having served in Malta, Sergeant Willetts was sent to Northern Ireland with his unit in January 1971.

The British Army presence in Northern Ireland at the start of the Troubles was initially to support the Royal Ulster Constabulary in upholding law and order. In 1971 protests and marches had given way to out-and-out violence and widespread public disorder. Army patrols were deeply unpopular and the first British soldier was killed on 6 February 1971.

3 Para were initially based in Armagh and moved later to West Belfast. On 25 May 1971, a terrorist entered the reception hall of Springfield Road Police Station in Belfast and dumped a suitcase on the floor before running off. A smoking fuse protruded from it. Already in the reception were four civilians (two of them children) and several police officers, one of whom immediately realised what had happened and raised the alarm. The police began to evacuate the building and Sergeant Willetts, who was on duty in the inner hall, sent an NCO upstairs to warn those above. Willetts held open the heavy door while the inhabitants of the building filed out, and stood in the doorway

> *All those approaching the door from the far side agree that if they had had to check to open the door they would have perished. Even when they had reached the rear passage, Sergeant Willetts waited, placing his body as a screen to shelter them. By this considered act of bravery, he risked – and lost – his life for those of the adults and children. His selflessness, his courage are beyond praise.*

in order to shield those who were rushing for cover. When the bomb exploded, Seargeant Willetts took the brunt of the force and was mortally wounded. His medal citation notes: 'All those approaching the door from the far side agree that if they had had to check to open the door they would have perished. Even when they had reached the rear passage, Sergeant Willetts waited, placing his body as a screen to shelter them. By this considered act of bravery, he risked – and lost – his life for those of the adults and children. His selflessness, his courage are beyond praise.'

An eyewitness later remarked on Willett's calmness and courage as he held the door open to allow people to evacuate the building.

The following month, Sergeant Willetts was awarded a posthumous GC, and 40 years later, his courage and gallantry are not forgotten. Every year on the anniversary of his death, a group of his comrades visit his grave in Nottinghamshire to pay tribute to his memory.

◀ *A British soldier injured in a bomb explosion in November 1971 is dragged to safety by his comrades.*

TROOPER SEKONAIA TAKAVESI

DCM

awarded 9 April 1974 • Oman • King's Own Royal Border Regiment/SAS

▼ Capturing hearts and minds – a trooper of the SAS gives medical treatment to the villagers of Falige, living in the remote Yanqul Plain of Oman, 1970.

Together with nine other men, Trooper Sekonaia Takavesi held off an attack by 250 heavily armed Omani tribesmen at the battle of Mirbat during the Dhofar Rebellion in 1972. He continued firing despite serious injuries, ensuring that the tribesmen were kept at bay until the arrival of reinforcements.

Sekonaia Takavesi ('Tak') was born in Fiji in 1943 and enlisted with the King's Own Royal Border Regiment (KORBR) in 1961. He joined 22 SAS in 1963, beginning a special forces career that was to last an astonishing 23 years. In addition to his valiant service in Oman, he was present at the Iranian Embassy Siege in London in 1980, and fought in the Falklands in 1982.

The Dhofar Rebellion was launched in 1962 from the southern dependency of Dhofar against the Sultanate of Muscat and Oman. The country was ruled by the despotic Sultan Said bin Taimur, who was utterly opposed to the progress offered by the twentieth century. Initially, the rebellion intended to overthrow him, but from 1967 it was backed by Communist forces that hoped to spread revolution throughout the Arabian peninsula. In 1970 the sultan's eldest son, Qaboos bin Said, launched a bloodless coup, and, backed by a small number of British special forces, began the long fight to gain control of his country.

From 1970 the SAS, designated as the British Army Training Team (BATT), trained government forces and embarked on a 'hearts and minds' campaign to win over the rebellious tribesmen – or People's Front for the Liberation of the Occupied Arabian Gulf (PFLOAG), better known to their enemies as 'Adoo'.

The rebel attack on the BATT house at Mirbat began at dawn on 19 July 1972, and immediately another Fijian, Corporal Labalaba, ran to operate the garrison's only 25-pounder gun, while the commander, Captain Mike Kealy, requested an air strike from headquarters in Salalah. When Labalaba was wounded, Takavesi sprinted the 500 yards (460m) to the gun pit, dressed his comrade's wound, and ran back to get more help. Returning to the gun pit with an Omani gunner, Takavesi picked off Adoo with his rifle, while the other two men operated the big gun. Soon, all three men were injured and, by the time Kealy and the company medic, Tommy Tobin, arrived, Labalaba was dead. Despite his own injuries, Takavesi continued firing.

The attack from the Adoo was relentless. Tobin was mortally injured and, just as it seemed as though they would be overwhelmed, two Omani Strikemaster jets flew over to bomb the enemy. At the same time, G Squadron arrived and cleared the Adoo from the local fort. The PFLOAG lost 40 dead, against two from the SAS, and their defeat to a force far smaller than their own destroyed their reputation.

When Tak finally arrived at hospital in Salalah, the surgeon announced that his chest wound was the worst he had ever seen on anyone who was still alive. Formidably fit, Tak survived, and was awarded the Distinguished Conduct Medal for his courage under fire.

▼ *Mirbat Fort, with the flag of Oman flying proudly from the roof. In 1972 this was garrisoned by 25 Omani paramilitary police equipped with elderly Lee-Enfield rifles. The bravery of the Fijians Labalaba and Takavesi in operating the 25-pounder ensured that the fort was not overrun by the enemy.*

RICHARD 'DICK' CRAIG
OBE, MC, CPM

awarded (MC) 10 May 1945 • Italy • 10th Baluchis/SIS

▼ *A view of Monte Cassino after heavy bombardment, showing a knocked-out Sherman tank by a Bailey bridge, with Monastery Ridge and Castle Hill in the background.*

Dick Craig had an extraordinary career of public service, receiving the Military Cross in Italy in 1944, serving as a highly respected colonial policeman in Malaya in the 1950s, and then joining the Secret Intelligence Service (SIS) in 1964.

Born in Limerick in 1921, Craig was one of twins (his brother went on to work as a film critic and writer) and was a talented rugby player. He gave up his medical studies at Trinity College Dublin to enlist in the British Army in 1941. Commissioned into the Indian Army, he commanded the 10th Baluchis during the invasion of Sicily. He proved to be a more than competent patrol leader, and ensured that he was thoroughly prepared for events by securing as much information as possible about the enemy. He led the Baluchis during the assault on Monte Cassino in February 1944, attacking Monastery Hill at the western end of the Gustav Line, and personally storming an enemy pillbox and killing the occupants. He was awarded the MC for his bravery and inspiring leadership.

Craig went on to fight in Greece in 1945, tackling the Communist-backed ELAS forces (the Greek People's Liberation Army) and briefly acting as a mayor of the town of Veria in Macedonia. After he was demobbed in 1946, Craig volunteered for service in the Palestine Police, but the task of trying to keep an uneasy peace between the Palestinians and the Jewish settlers proved to be difficult, thankless and dangerous.

In Malaya in 1948, Dick Craig joined the Federation Police, just as the Malayan Emergency was beginning. His habit of meticulous preparation and his razor-sharp mind equipped him perfectly for the job of intelligence-gathering. Craig ran agents and informers through the jungle networks, and ensured that intelligence, once gathered, was acted upon immediately by the army. His work with the intelligence branch of the police was very highly rated and he was 'an absolutely first rate policeman from Limerick', according to General Sir Gerald Templer, the High Commissioner of Malaya from 1952 to 1954. Craig wrote an account of his work in Malaya that was never published, but was consulted by American analysts striving to improve their intelligence-gathering in Vietnam.

He retired from his position as Head of Special Branch in Malaya in 1964, having been awarded both an OBE in 1962 for his valuable work, and the Colonial Police Medal. In search of more foreign adventures, Craig joined the SIS in 1964. He was sent to the Gulf States for three years from 1966, where Britain wanted to retain influence as the various states adapted to the almighty change in their fortunes brought about by oil wealth. He worked in Delhi from 1973 to 1975, again smoothing the path of British diplomacy in the face of increasing Soviet influence in the subcontinent. He also served in London, working in personnel and security.

Craig projected the image of a bluff, friendly Irishman, but this concealed a shrewd mind and an aptitude for assessing situations and people. He died in 2000 and was remembered with enormous respect and great fondness by those who had worked with him.

▼ *A Humber armoured car supports paratroops during operations against ELAS in Athens, 6 January 1945.*

ADMIRAL OF THE FLEET SIR MICHAEL POLLOCK

GCB, LVO, DSC

awarded (DSC) 1944 • Battle of North Cape • Royal Navy

When Admiral Sir Michael Pollock retired in 1974, it was after a career stretching back more than 40 years, during which he was awarded the Distinguished Service Cross for his part in the sinking of the *Scharnhorst* in 1943, and rose to be First Sea Lord.

▼ The First Sea Lord, Admiral Sir Michael Pollock, presenting the White Ensign to Rear Admiral Morgan-Giles, Chairman of the HMS Belfast Trust, at the ship's opening ceremony, 21 October 1971.

Michael Pollock was born in 1916 and entered Dartmouth as a 13-year old cadet in 1930, before being commissioned as a midshipman in 1933. When war broke out, he was appointed first lieutenant aboard the destroyer HMS

Vanessa, escorting military convoys across the Atlantic, and he spent most of the war in convoy protection. He trained as a gunnery specialist in 1941, and was mentioned in dispatches for his role as gunnery officer aboard HMS *Arethusa* in 1942, when the ship was hit by a Junkers 88 torpedo bomber.

Pollock was promoted to lieutenant commander, and in 1943 was appointed gunnery officer aboard the heavy cruiser HMS *Norfolk,* which took part in the Royal Navy's last battleship action at the Battle of North Cape in December 1943. In heavy seas and bitter weather, *Norfolk* was shelled by *Scharnhorst,* and lost a turret and her radar, but Pollock managed to continue to fire directly on the German cruiser, hitting *Scharnhorst's* radar aerial and contributing significantly to the ship's ultimate demise. He was awarded the DSC for his gallant and dedicated action.

After the war, Pollock was appointed Lieutenant of the Royal Victorian Order (LVO)

for his part in the organisation of King George VI's funeral. He saw action off Korea aboard the cruiser HMS *Newcastle,* and by 1954 was second-in-command of the Far East Fleet. In 1963 he commanded the aircraft carrier HMS *Ark Royal* when it carried out trials with the new Harrier jump jets.

As Assistant Chief of Naval Staff from 1964 to 1966, he had his first taste of the reality of high-level budgetary arguments, as the 1966 Defence White Paper threatened the future of naval fixed-wing aviation. His last seagoing appointment was as second-in-command of the Home Fleet, aboard the cruiser HMS *Tiger,* which, in 1966, became the site of the 'Tiger talks' between Prime Minister Harold Wilson and the premier of Rhodesia, Ian Smith, over the country's future.

Pollock's next appointment in 1968, as Flag Officer Submarines, was something of a surprise, as he was a gunnery officer and not a submariner, but it was clear that he was being groomed for a position on the Admiralty Board. It was an interesting period, as the Polaris fleet was embedded as Britain's primary weapon of nuclear deterrence.

As controller of the Navy from 1970, Pollock was responsible for ship design and construction at a time when the fleet was being re-shaped and Britain was reducing its global naval role. He was unexpectedly promoted to First Sea Lord in 1971, and the last three years of his career were by no means a gentle coast to retirement, encompassing as they did the Cod War with Iceland, the 1974 oil crisis, and radical defence cuts.

▲ *The battle of North Cape, December 1943.*

▼ *HMS* Norfolk *earned an impressive set of battle honours during the Second World War and was involved in sinking some of the most famous ships of the Kriegsmarine, including the Bismarck in 1941 and Scharnhorst in 1943.*

CAPTAIN PETER LAKE
MC, CROIX DE GUERRE

awarded 21 June 1945 • Occupied France • SOE

▼ A member of the French Resistance sets an explosive charge on a railway line. Lake trained a team of the Resistance in sabotage techniques in 1944.

Peter Lake was a skilled linguist, a talent that underwrote both his long post-war career as a diplomat, and his wartime missions with the Special Operations Executive (SOE).

Born in 1915 and brought up on Majorca, where his father was British consul, Peter Lake grew up bilingual in English and Spanish. He studied Modern Languages at St John's College, Oxford, before embarking on a banking career in the colonies. When war broke out, he was working in the Standard Bank in Accra, Ghana, but he made his way back to England overland just as the troops that had been evacuated from Dunkirk were arriving in ports all along the south coast.

Lake volunteered for the army, and was swiftly placed in the Intelligence Corps, where his linguistic skills could be used to best effect. He joined the SOE and in 1942 was sent back to West Africa as vice-consul on the Spanish island of Ferdinand Pó off the coast of Cameroon.

When the Italian ship *Duchessa d'Aosta* arrived in harbour, Lake saw the opportunity to score a point against the Axis powers. Using his considerable diplomatic skills, combined with good old-fashioned bribery and low cunning, Lake put in place a plan to lure most of the ship's crew into town on a particular night, leaving only a skeleton crew aboard the ship, which could then be captured by a boarding party he had organised to arrive from Lagos. Lake's plan worked perfectly: the *Duchessa* was captured, then sailed out to sea and deliberately 'intercepted' by HMS *Violet*. The ship was accompanied back to England, providing a valuable morale boost at a particularly low point of the war for Britain.

Lake returned to England in August 1943 and underwent further training with the SOE, including a signals course. His service record at this time notes that he was 'more academic than practical', although 'he has plenty of common sense and is well able to look after himself'.

In April 1944, Peter Lake was dropped behind enemy lines in France with the aim of organising and training Resistance groups in advance of the Allied invasion. His course included 'evening classes in sabotage' and 'a

week-long commando course'. His leadership of the *Maquis* was initially difficult, as he had to persuade a disparate group of veterans of the Spanish Civil War to take instruction in the use of explosives. But he quickly gained their respect and his unit had a number of successes, including the destruction of the main railway line to Perigeaux after D-Day. His 'excellent service in preparing and directing the local resistance activities in support of the Allied invasion and his courage in leading repeated attacks on enemy targets' earned him a Military Cross. He was also awarded the Croix de Guerre, in spite of being snubbed by an irascible General de Gaulle in September 1944, who resented what he regarded as excessive British influence over 'his' Free French.

After the war, Lake worked for the consular service around the world, before retiring in 1975, when he worked for the Cambridge Wildlife Trust.

▲ *Peter Lake as a young officer in the Intelligence Corps during the Second World War.*

A corporal from the 3rd Battalion the Light Infantry passes
ruined terraced houses during a patrol of one of the Peace
Lines in Belfast in 1977. The Peace Lines were a series of street
barriers separating republican and loyalist communities, erected
in the early 1970s in an attempt to minimise sectarian violence
in Northern Ireland.

FLIGHT LIEUTENANT MICHELLE GOODMAN
DFC

awarded 7 March 2008 • Iraq • RAF

▼ *At the Remembrance Day Parade in 2008, some of Britain's newly decorated heroes, including Michelle Goodman, join surviving First World War veterans to lay wreaths at the Cenotaph on the 90th anniversary of the first Armistice Service.*

A skilful and courageous pilot, Flight Lieutenant Goodman is the first woman to be awarded the Distinguished Flying Cross. She has carried out three tours of duty in Iraq, has served in Afghanistan, and was awarded the DFC for rescuing an injured serviceman while under fire from the enemy.

Born in Bristol in 1976, Michelle Goodman had long harboured an ambition to be a pilot. After gaining a Master's degree in Aerospace Engineering, she was accepted for officer training at Cranwell in May 2000. She began training as a helicopter pilot at RAF Shawbury and, as a flight lieutenant, joined No. 28 Squadron at RAF Benson in 2004.

Goodman was trained to fly Merlin helicopters, the RAF's medium lift transport and utility helicopter. In March 2005, Goodman travelled with the rest of No. 28 Squadron to Basra Air Station in southern Iraq, as part of Operation Telic. She completed a further two tours of duty in Iraq, and it was on the last, in June 2007, that she took part in the rescue that resulted in the award.

Merlins are all-weather, day-and-night, multi-role helicopters, adaptable to almost any role within the RAF, and as such are something of a workhorse. They are used for transporting personnel or injured combatants, for surveillance, or for taking the fight direct to the enemy, with a small squadron of airborne heli-snipers. They can act as the eyes of ground forces, are proven deterrents in the face of the enemy, and provide critical support to troops on the ground as instant reaction teams (IRTs).

It was in this last role that Flight Lieutenant Goodman took off on 1 June 2007. Her team was asked to retrieve a casualty seriously injured in a mortar attack in the centre of Basra City at 2315 hours. It was undoubtedly a high-risk operation. Forced to fly at a comparatively low altitude across a hostile city, Goodman was flying with night-vision goggles in poor visibility, and the helicopter was exposed to enemy fire as it came in to land on a small, obstructed site. 'I think this could be a bit dodgy,' she remarked to her team, who were all well aware of the dangers. The dust was so bad that she had to be guided the last 20 metres to the ground by the crew. It took five minutes for the medics to locate and retrieve the casualty, and although Goodman kept the rotors turning, the helicopter was an open target. Once the casualty had been brought on board, Goodman took off, just as four RPGs whizzed towards them. Incredibly, they were back at the base just 14 minutes after the initial call-out.

Michelle Goodman's medal citation underlines her skill as an outstanding pilot: 'Without the IRT, the casualty would have died within 15 minutes. Despite extreme pressure, whilst in the face of the enemy, she made the right decision. This was a bold and daring sortie which undoubtedly saved life.'

She has also used her celebrity as the RAF's most highly decorated female pilot to raise charitable funds for military causes such as Help for Heroes and the National Memorial Arboretum, linked to the Royal British Legion.

> *Without the IRT, the casualty would have died within 15 minutes. Despite extreme pressure, whilst in the face of the enemy, she made the right decision. This was a bold and daring sortie which undoubtedly saved life.*

▶ *Flight Lieutenant Michelle Goodman, DFC.*

SERGEANT HENRY TANDEY
VC, DCM, MM

awarded (VC) 1918 • Western Front • Duke of Wellington's (West Riding Regiment)

Henry Tandey, who died in 1977, was the most highly decorated private soldier of the First World War. Mentioned in dispatches on five separate occasions, he was also awarded the Distinguished Conduct Medal, the Military Medal and finally the Victoria Cross for his actions during the Battle of the Canal du Nord at the end of September 1918.

▼ *Henry Tandey's medals, including the VC on the left, are displayed in the Green Howards regimental museum in Richmond, North Yorkshire.*

Henry Tandey was born in Leamington, Warwickshire, in 1891 and joined the pre-war Regular British Army in 1910. He enlisted in the Green Howards and served with them in South Africa prior to the start of the First World War.

He served with the 2nd Battalion during the Battle of First Ypres in 1914, as well as on the Somme in 1916, where he was wounded in the leg. Following his recovery he was posted to the 9th Battalion, with whom he was wounded again in 1917 during the Battle of Passchendaele.

In July 1918 he was transferred from the Green Howards to the 5th Battalion The Duke of Wellington's Regiment, with whom he served until the end of the war. It was with this regiment that he earned his major honours during the Hundred Days Campaign that led to the signing of the Armistice on 11 November 1918. First, he was awarded the DCM for his actions during the battle for Vaulx-Vraucourt on 28 August 1918, when he led his reserve bombing party forward under fire and captured 20 prisoners. He then went on to be awarded the MM for his part in the attack on Havrincourt on 12 September, when he once more led a bombing party forward and captured a large number of prisoners.

On 28 September his battalion was involved in fighting around Marcoing as part of the operation to force a crossing of the Canal du Nord just outside the city of Cambrai. When Tandey's platoon was held up by machine-gun fire, he crawled forward and located the position, before silencing it with a Lewis gun team. He then went forward, while still under fire, to repair the plank bridge and allow the rest of his platoon to move forward. When the inevitable German counterattack materialised, he and eight other men were surrounded by a much larger party of Germans, so Tandey led a bayonet charge that drove them back, with 37 being captured. During all of this Tandey was wounded twice and refused treatment until the battle was over. For this he was awarded the VC.

Following the end of the war he stayed in the army, being promoted to sergeant and serving in Turkey, Gibraltar and Egypt.

▼ *A group of German prisoners taken at the Battle of Amiens in August 1918, the start of a series of victories for the Allies in the run-up to the end of the war in November.*

GENERAL SIR RUPERT SMITH KCB
DSO AND BAR, OBE, QGM

awarded (QGM) 7 August 1978 • Northern Ireland • Parachute Regiment

One of the most experienced generals of his generation, Rupert Smith saw service in almost every area of conflict from his time as a junior officer in the Parachute Regiment in the 1960s, to his final appointment as Deputy Supreme Allied Commander Europe. In addition, since his retirement he has proved to be a formidable military thinker, producing a thought-provoking book, *The Utility of Force*, a treatise on the changing nature of modern warfare.

▼ An artist's impression of the massed forces of the coalition that lined up to fight Saddam Hussain in 1990–91. General Smith led the British force.

Rupert Smith was born in 1943 and was commissioned as a second lieutenant in the parachute regiment in 1964 after graduating from Sandhurst. By 1978 he was a company commander serving in South Armagh, Northern Ireland, during the very difficult years of the Troubles. Caught up in a car bomb blast, he somehow pulled his platoon commander Lieutenant David Leigh from the flaming vehicle, despite a heat so fierce that his radio melted. Smith acted instinctively to smother the flames on his comrade, without thinking about his own safety, and was awarded the Queen's Gallantry Medal for his actions.

Smith has proved time and again that he is not only a brave man but also a thoughtful and focused military leader. Promotions followed swiftly in the 1980s, and in 1990 he was appointed major general in command of the 1st Armoured Division. He led the 35,000-strong division during the First Gulf War (1990–91), a huge and complex undertaking as head of the largest British armoured force deployed in action since the Second World War. Smith rose to the challenge of uniting and training his division in just six weeks and was awarded the Distinguished Service Order for his exceptional leadership and personal bravery.

As Assistant Chief of Defence Operations and Security at the MOD from 1992, he became involved in strategic planning for the UK's involvement in Bosnia-Herzegovina and in 1995 he was appointed Commander of the Bosnia and Herzegovina Command as an acting lieutenant general. Sent to Sarajevo, then in the grips of a brutal siege, he was responsible for ensuring that humanitarian relief reached the city, but was frustrated by the lack of political will to cut short the military atrocities. He forcefully maintained the 'safe areas' and was ultimately responsible for breaking the siege and ending the war. His outstanding work was rewarded by a second DSO.

After two years as General Officer Commanding Northern Ireland (1996–98), he returned to the Balkans as Deputy Supreme Allied Commander Europe, covering the NATO operation during the Kosovo conflict. He retired from the army in 2002 and since then has earned a reputation as radical military commentator. His book, *The Utility of Force*, was published in 2005 and explains how the nature of warfare has altered, while modern western armies have not kept pace with the changes.

Intelligent, courageous, and apparently fearless in his criticism, now that he has been released from his military commission, General Sir Rupert Smith is a logical thinker whose matchless military experience means that serving politicians and generals might give serious consideration to his observations about the use of force in the twenty-first century.

▼ *Rupert Smith pictured when he commanded 1st (UK) Armoured Division during the First Gulf War (1990–91).*

CAPTAIN ROBERT NAIRAC
GC

awarded 13 February 1979 • Northern Ireland • Grenadier Guards

Grenadier Guards officer Captain Robert Nairac was posthumously awarded the George Cross in 1979 for his role in military intelligence in Northern Ireland. Abducted in a pub car park by the IRA, he was tortured and then murdered without revealing his true identity or mission to his captors. His immense courage in not divulging intelligence under torture surely saved others' lives.

Robert Nairac was born in Mauritius in 1948, the son of an eye surgeon. He attended Ampleforth College, before reading history at Oxford and then going on to enter Sandhurst. He was recognised to be a highly intelligent

young man, with wide-ranging interests and great sporting prowess as a boxing blue at Oxford. He was fascinated by Ireland, partly because his family had Irish roots, and partly because he had spent time there with close

▶ *Captain Robert Nairac talking to children in the Ardoyne area of Belfast, February 1977.*

◀ Two years after his death, members of the Nairac family – (from left) Maurice, Barbara and their daughter Rosamonde – were presented with the GC in Robert's honour on 2 May 1979.

▼ A formal portrait of Captain Robert Nairac in the uniform of the Grenadier Guards.

friends in Dublin and Galway. He was also a devout Roman Catholic.

After completing his training at Sandhurst, Nairac studied for a postgraduate degree at University College Dublin before operational duties with the Grenadier Guards, using his time to immerse himself in Irish culture. His unit, No. 1 Company 2nd Battalion Grenadier Guards, was deployed to Northern Ireland on 5 July 1973, remaining until the end of October that year. Just a year after the Bloody Sunday massacre, the relations between the Protestant and Catholic communities were still extremely tense and the battalion's primary objective was to search for both weapons and paramilitary soldiers. They also mingled with the community in an effort to break down the barriers between the military and the local population, and Nairac particularly enjoyed working with young people in the Catholic Ardoyne area of Belfast.

Nairac had a true passion for Ireland, and when the rest of the regiment was due to be posted to Hong Kong, he volunteered for military intelligence duties. He returned to the mainland for specialist training at the Army Joint Intelligence College in Kent, and for an SAS training course designed specifically for operations in Northern Ireland.

He returned to the Province in 1974 and carried out surveillance duties as part of 14th Intelligence Company (14 INT). It appears that he also took it upon himself to visit known republican pubs, presumably in an effort to infiltrate IRA networks.

During his fourth tour of duty on 14 May 1977, Nairac visited a republican pub in South Armagh, posing as an IRA member from north Belfast. He was abducted from the pub car park and taken across the border where he was interrogated, tortured and killed. His disappearance prompted an intense four-day military search.

During his ordeal, Nairac refused to give away any details concerning his military duties or the names of his comrades, and in the words of his medal citation, 'These efforts to break Captain Nairac's will failed entirely'. He was murdered by an IRA gunman, but demonstrated exceptional courage and heroism. Even his captors were impressed. His killer later said, 'He was the bravest man I ever met. He told us nothing. He was a good soldier.'

Captain Robert Nairac was awarded a posthumous GC two years after his death, in 1979.

SERGEANT PETE WINNER

Iranian Embassy Siege • SAS

Although he has no formal decorations for gallantry, Pete Winner served with the SAS for 18 years and saw action at the famous Battle of Mirbat in 1972, as well as the operation to break the Iranian Embassy Siege in 1980, before going on to serve in the Falklands in 1982.

Pete Winner was serving with the Royal Engineers in Aden in 1967 when he first became aware of the SAS. Inspired to join, he underwent the fearsome selection process and qualified in 1969, going to serve with B Squadron in the fighting against the communist rebels in the Dhofar region of Oman. It was here that Winner took part in the fabled Battle of Mirbat, where nine members of the SAS held off a much larger force of rebels in a desperate action.

Promoted to sergeant, Winner later served in Northern Ireland and Hong Kong, following which he was returned to the Royal Engineers for 12 months for disciplinary reasons before passing selection once more in January 1979 and returning to the SAS, though as a trooper once more. He was just in time to take part in one of the most famous of the regiment's operations, the crushing of the Iranian Embassy Siege in 1980.

▶ Pete Winner on his first operational tour with the SAS, Operation Jaguar – the battle to control the mountainous Jebel Massif in Dhofar, Oman.

On 30 April 1980, six Iraqi-backed Iranian revolutionaries had burst into the Iranian Embassy in Princes Gate, just to the south of Hyde Park. Taking over the embassy, the terrorists took 26 hostages. Over the course of the following days, the situation grew increasingly tense as police negotiators sought to break the deadlock.

On the sixth day of the siege, Monday 5 May, the terrorists executed one of the hostages, which was the signal for the operation to become a matter for the SAS rather than the police, and plans were immediately put into effect to bring the siege to a conclusion. Just after 7.20pm the assault went in, with SAS teams abseiling from the roof of the Embassy and breaking in through the upper-floor windows. Pete Winner's team was next door and immediately broke in through the back of the embassy. Having cleared the cellar and ground floor, which were both unoccupied, they helped to evacuate the hostages from the embassy. While doing this, Winner spotted one of the terrorists among the hostages, and knocked him down with the butt of his weapon to stop him using a grenade. The terrorist was then neutralised by troopers at the bottom of the stairs.

The operation had been a major success, with only one of the hostages killed by the terrorists during the assault, although a further two were wounded. The SAS suffered one serious injury, while only one terrorist survived the siege.

▼ The SAS assault party on the second-floor balcony of the Iranian Embassy. On the far left, the trooper has had his gas-mask and hood burned off.

CHAPTER SEVEN

1981–1990 A need for change

▼ *Mrs Sara Jones, widow of Lieutenant Colonel 'H' Jones VC, launches the 1983 Poppy Appeal. She later became Chairman of the Poppy Factory.*

The Conservative Government of 1979 came to power with promises to cut inflation, and they set about doing this by restricting the money supply by raising interest rates, cutting public spending, and raising taxes to deal with the deficit that had built up in the 1970s. These policies had the effect of causing a massive drop in manufacturing and led to a great rise in unemployment. The rising number of unemployed, containing inevitably a large number of ex-servicemen, meant that there was much work for the Legion to do. Increasingly, the Legion was now dealing with those who had suffered in the many post-war conflicts in which the British Army had been involved. Since 1945 the British armed forces had suffered 4000 killed and 16 000 wounded, and the casualties and their dependants all needed the support of the Legion. In addition, in 1981 the Legion decided to allow serving members of the armed forces to join as ordinary members – before this they had been able to use Legion facilities only as honorary members. However, the focus of the Legion's benevolent work was to remain on the eight million ex-servicemen and ex-servicewomen and their ten million dependants.

The profile of the armed services and the Legion was raised following the Falklands War of 1982, which brought the realities of conflict into the nation's living rooms. British casualties were happily low, but nevertheless, the massive public response to the conflict and great pride in the armed forces' achievements, led to an outpouring of donations, in particular to the South Atlantic Fund, though the Legion as ever recognised the need to plan for the long-term needs of those involved in the campaign.

The late 1980s saw the end of the Cold War that had plagued the world since the end of the Second World War in 1945. The collapse of the Soviet Empire throughout Eastern Europe led to what became known as the 'peace dividend', as Western governments took the opportunity to reduce their commitment to defence spending. Inevitably this necessitated redundancies among the armed forces, and the Legion became much more involved in the resettlement and training of ex-servicemen.

However, all of this new work required money, and the Legion was still struggling to

1981	1982	1983	1984	1985
The Legion allows serving armed forces personnel to join as ordinary members for the first time	The Falklands War brings the reality of modern conflict home to the nation		Establishment of the Legion's Pilgrimages Department to provide trips to graves and memorials abroad	Legion Housing Association completes its 11 500th flat let

◀ *Throughout the 1980s the Legion made increasing use of famous personalities to promote the Poppy Appeal and its other charitable activities. Here, the badly burned Falklands War veteran Simon Weston plants a cross in soil flown especially from Goose Green at the launch of the 1986 Poppy Appeal.*

▼ *The Queen Mother speaks to ex-servicemen, during her walkabout at the annual Field of Remembrance Service outside Westminster Abbey, after she placed her own personal small wooden cross on a waist-height stand on the edge of a lawn planted with thousands of other tiny wooden crosses bearing Royal British Legion poppies.*

attract funding in what was an increasingly competitive market for charities. The Legion came 16th among the UK's charities in terms of income, with Oxfam heading the list, and the second half of the 1980s would see the return of difficult times for some of the Legion's institutions, particularly those clubs in the north and north-west, where unemployment was particularly rife.

The collapse in property prices in the late 1980s also brought disaster to the Legion Leasehold Housing Association, which had been set up in 1981 to help ex-service people buy sheltered housing. This went into receivership, owing £1 million to the Legion, of which only

£300 000 was recovered. A critical Charity Commission report on the collapse provided more impetus for the Legion to change. This process was already underway with the computerisation and centralisation of Legion records, enabling it to better market its service to its members. Management consultants were also called in and a thorough review of the Legion's structures and services was undertaken in time for the new decade.

| 1986 | 1987 | 1988 | 1989 | 1990 |

Collapse of the Legion Leasehold Housing Association leads to internal reform

GENERAL SIR MICHAEL ROSE
KCB, CBE, DSO, QGM

awarded (QGM) 1981 • Princess Gate • Coldstream Guards/SAS

General Sir Michael Rose is one of Britain's most distinguished generals, having commanded the SAS from 1979 to 1982, and served as the Director, Special Forces (1988–89). He was awarded the Queen's Gallantry Medal for his role in ending the Iranian Embassy siege in London in 1980. He went on to command the United Nations Protection Force in Bosnia.

▶ *General Sir Michael Rose, Commanding Officer United Nations Forces, Bosnia, during a press conference at which he unveiled plans to conduct air strikes against Serb positions around Sarajevo if they did not hand in their heavy weapons, February 1994.*

A child of empire, and stepson of the Raj novelist John Masters, Rose was born in Quetta, India in 1940. He began his military career in the Territorial Army, before being commissioned into the Coldstream Guards in 1964. It is uncertain when he passed the rigorous selection board for the SAS, but Rose was a captain with the 1st Battalion the Coldstream Guards in 1971–72, and was present in Londonderry during the infamous Bloody Sunday massacre.

After attending Staff College, he became brigade major of the 16th Parachute Brigade from 1973 to 1975. As a Special Forces soldier, the fine details of Rose's career are still shrouded in secrecy, but he served in Germany, Aden, Malaysia, the Gulf States, Dhofar, Northern Ireland, the Falkland Islands and the Balkans.

Rose was commanding officer of 22 SAS Regiment from 1979 to 1982, a period that encompassed two of the regiment's finest hours. On 30 May 1980 terrorists took over the Iranian Embassy in London, and captured 22 hostages. For five days there was a tense stalemate between British government negotiators and the terrorists, until on 5 May control was handed to Lieutenant Colonel Michael Rose. Rose immediately implemented a rescue attempt, which was carried out by black-clad SAS soldiers trained in hostage rescue. It was the most high-profile event in the Regiment's history and Rose was awarded the QGM for his part.

The following year, under Rose's command, the SAS played an important part in recapturing the Falkland Islands after the Argentinean invasion, working alongside the Royal Marines and the Special Boat Service. Rose earned a Mentioned in Dispatches and took part in the final negotiations which led to the Argentine surrender.

During the 1980s, Rose commanded 39 Infantry Brigade in Northern Ireland (1983–85),

and attended the Royal College of Defence Studies in 1986, before becoming the first Director, Special Forces in 1988. In January 1994 he took command of the United Nations Protection Force (UNPROFOR) in Bosnia-Herzegovina, an immensely complex job that was not without controversy.

A cerebral soldier whose operational expertise is highly valued, Rose reached one of the highest ranks of his profession when he was appointed Adjutant General of the army in 1995, his last military command before retirement in 1997. Since his retirement, he has lectured extensively on peace-keeping and leadership. He has published two books, *Fighting for Peace* in 1998, about the war in Bosnia, and *Washington's War* in 2007, comparing the American War of Independence with the US-led war in Iraq.

▼ *Members of the SAS enter the Iranian Embassy on 5 May 1980, to end a six-day siege in central London. Nineteen hostages were rescued, and three gunmen shot dead.*

LIEUTENANT GENERAL SIR JOHN PANTON KISZELY

KCB, MC

awarded 8 October 1982 • Falklands • Scots Guards

Sir John Kiszely is the current National President of the Royal British Legion, a role he took up in December 1998. Prior to that he had a distinguished military career, during which he was awarded the Military Cross for his actions as a company commander of the Scots Guards during the Falklands War of 1982.

▼ Men of the 2nd Battalion Scots Guards on Tumbledown celebrate the news of the Argentine surrender at dawn on 14 June 1982.

Kiszely entered the army straight from Marlborough College in 1969, and served with the Scots Guards in Northern Ireland and Germany before the Argentine invasion of the Falklands Islands in 1982.

By this time, Kiszely was a major in command of the Left Flank Company of the 2nd Battalion Scots Guards, and the battalion was sent south to the Falklands Islands as part of 5th Infantry Brigade, the second wave of troops that arrived in San Carlos on 2 June. The Brigade was immediately committed to the capture of the Island's capital, Port Stanley. Stanley was ringed by a series of mountainous positions, all occupied by Argentine troops, and the British had to break through this ring to get through to Stanley. The 5th Infantry Brigade was moved by sea to positions at Bluff Cove and Fitzroy from 6 to 8 June. On 8 June, the *Sir Galahad*, carrying the Welsh Guards, was hit by the Argentine Air Force, causing great loss of life. On the night of 12/13 June, the troops of 3 Commando Brigade cleared the outer ring of mountains, Mount Harriet, Two Sisters and Mount Longdon, and, following a day's

▲ *Lieutenant General Sir John Panton Kiszely, the current National President of the Royal British Legion.*

> *Despite men falling wounded beside him he continued his charge, throwing grenades as he went. Arriving on the enemy position, he killed two enemy with his rifle and a third with his bayonet. His courageous action forced the surrender of the remainder.*

delay to re-stock artillery ammunition, the Scots Guards and 1/7th Gurkhas moved into position to assault the remaining obstacles: Tumbledown and Mount William.

Following a diversionary attack, Major Kiszely's Left Flank Company were about halfway up the ridge when they ran into the main Argentine position and became pinned down by heavy fire, remaining with their heads down for three hours. Realising that his men were starting to become incapacitated by the cold, Major Kiszely gathered together all the company's anti-tank weapons and renewed the assault, overrunning the Argentine positions one after another. Kiszely himself was closely involved in the fighting, and ended up in hand-to-hand fighting with the enemy, as his citation makes clear: 'Despite men falling wounded beside him he continued his charge, throwing grenades as he went. Arriving on the enemy position, he killed two enemy with his rifle and a third with his bayonet. His courageous action forced the surrender of the remainder.' By the time they reached the top of Tumbledown, only six men were with Kiszely, but the ridge had fallen and the road to Stanley lay open.

▼ *Walking wounded of the Scots Guards move towards a scout helicopter for evacuation.*

BRIGADIER SIR JOHN SMYTH
VC, MC, PC

awarded (VC) 29 June 1915 • Western Front • 15th Ludhiana Sikhs

▼ *Sir John Smyth's collection of gallantry and campaign medals from both world wars. The VC is at far left, followed by the MC. His medals were donated to the Imperial War Museum following his death and are on display there.*

John Smyth, who passed away in April 1983, was awarded the Victoria Cross while serving with the Indian Army on the Western Front during the Battle of Festubert in May 1915. He went on to serve with distinction in the Second World War, before becoming a member of parliament in the post-war years.

John Smyth was born in Devon and attended Sandhurst before being commissioned into the 15th Ludhiana Sikhs, part of the Indian Army in 1912. Following service in India, his battalion was committed to the fighting on the Western Front after the outbreak of the First World War in 1914, arriving in September 1914. In May 1915 they were in the front line during the Battle of Festubert, part of the Artois offensive. Lieutenant Smyth was the officer in charge of bombing for

the battalion and, on 18 May, he was charged with resupplying a company of the 15th Sikhs that had taken a section of German trench and was running low on ammunition and grenades and in danger of being overrun.

Two attempts to resupply this force had failed with heavy losses, but Smyth took along ten volunteers and made another attempt. Immediately confronted by heavy German fire, the party crawled along a disused stretch of trench with nine of the party being killed or wounded. Smyth and one other pushed forwards with a box of grenades, fording across a deep stream until they eventually reached the surprised defenders of the captured trench. The delivered grenades ensured that the position could be held until nightfall, when Smyth returned to his position, having been given up for dead.

He was awarded the VC for his bravery, and went on to serve in Egypt and Mesopotamia. Smyth later received the MC for operations in Waziristan in 1919 and held high command during the Second World War, commanding

a brigade during the Fall of France and evacuation from Dunkirk, as well as the 17th Indian Division during the early days of the Japanese campaign against Burma.

Following the end of the war he served as a Conservative MP for 16 years. He was also involved in the founding of the Victoria Cross and George Cross Association in 1956, becoming the association's first chairman and serving as its life president from 1971 until his death.

◄ John Smyth earned the VC during the Battle of Festubert on 18 May 1915. He later served with his battalion in Egypt and Mesopotamia, before going on to higher command during the Second World War.

LIEUTENANT COMMANDER HAROLD NEWGASS
GC

awarded 4 March 1941 • The Blitz • RNVR

Harold Newgass, who died in 1984, was awarded the George Cross for one of the most hazardous bomb disposal operations of the Blitz. Working in desperate conditions, he managed to successfully defuse a German mine that had threatened the gas supply for much of the city of Liverpool.

▼ The electro-mechanical fuse timer removed from the parachute mine that fell through the large gasometer at Garston gasworks in Liverpool on 28 November 1940 – the mine that was made safe by Lieutenant Harold Newgass.

Harold Newgass was born and brought up in London and had served with the Territorial Army during the First World War, and although he was sent to France he did not reach the front line before the end of the war. He remained in the Territorials until 1934, and on the outbreak of the Second World War he joined the Royal Naval Volunteer Reserve. While he was undergoing training he signed up for special duties, bomb disposal work for the Torpedo and Mining Department.

The German aerial bombardment known as the Blitz was launched in September 1940, and there was plenty of work for bomb disposal teams. Liverpool, as an important port city, was one of the principal targets of German attacks and suffered heavily at the end of November. Lieutenant Newgass was sent there with his team to clear unexploded ordnance.

On 28 November a German parachute mine had fallen through the roof of a gasholder at the Garston gasworks, causing 6000 people to be evacuated from their homes, and threatening the gas supply to half of Liverpool. This was a large weapon designed to explode at roof height and cause widespread damage, destroying perhaps a street of houses at one time. Realising that defusing this mine would be an arduous and extremely dangerous task, Newgass elected to take on the task alone.

The gas-laden atmosphere was unbreathable, so Newgass was provided with oxygen cylinders by the local fire brigade, each of which lasted for 30 minutes. Once the water surrounding the mine had been pumped away, he began his

◀ Harold Newgass in his uniform as an officer in the Royal Naval Volunteer Reserve.

▼ Smoking rubble after a German bombing raid on Liverpool in December 1940.

attempt to defuse the mine. It took him nearly three hours and six oxygen-fuelled trips, to make the mine safe, as he first assessed the situation, then transported his tools and equipment, before lashing the mine to supports. He then carefully turned the mine into position and finally removed the clock, rendering it safe. For this dangerous task he was awarded the GC 'for great gallantry and undaunted devotion to duty'. The gasworks, employees and local residents all gave him presents to convey their personal thanks for his role, one that he would continue in for the next four years, rising to the rank of lieutenant commander, until he was found to be medically unfit to carry on.

FIELD MARSHAL EDWIN BRAMALL, BARON BRAMALL

KG, GCB, OBE, MC, DL, JP

awarded (MC) 1 March 1945 • Northwest Europe • King's Royal Rifle Corps

▼ British chiefs of staff during the Falklands War – General Sir Edwin Bramall (Chief of General Staff) is pictured in the centre foreground.

Field Marshal Edwin Bramall retired from his post as Chief of the Defence Staff in 1985. Most famous as the senior officer in the British Army during the Falklands War, he served as a junior officer in the 2nd Battalion The King's Royal Rifle Corps during the campaign in Northwest Europe 1944–45, where he was awarded the Military Cross.

Edwin Bramall joined the army in 1943 straight out of Eton, going into the 2nd Battalion The King's Royal Rifle Corps (2 KRRC), a regiment that had already seen much action in the war. 2 KRRC had originally consisted of two regular battalions, the 1st and 2nd, and a further six territorial battalions, the 7th, 8th, 9th, 10th, 11th and 12th. The 2nd and 7th had both been lost in their entirety at the fall of Calais in 1940, while the 1st, the reconstituted 2nd, and the 9th battalions had served with distinction in the Desert War. The 1st Battalion had originally been under the command of the great desert officer Lieutenant Colonel W. F. E. Gott, MC, and part of the fabled 7th Armoured Division, the original 'Desert Rats'. The 2nd Battalion had served with 4th Armoured Division in north Africa and Italy, and was withdrawn back to the UK to train for the Normandy landings.

◀ A universal carrier of 12th King's Royal Rifle Corps in action against a German machine-gun position in Holland on 2 April 1945. 12 KRRC was part of 8th Armoured Brigade and took part in many of the same campaigns as 2 KRRC.

Going ashore on 7 June, the day after D-Day, 2 KRRC fought its way through the Normandy campaign, taking part in the action around Falaise and pushing on into Belgium after the retreating German forces. By the autumn, following the failure of Operation Market Garden, the front was relatively stable and 2 KRRC spent the autumn and winter on operations in north-east Holland, where Lieutenant Edwin Bramall earned his MC for his actions around the village of Poppel on 20 October 1944.

Placed in charge of a reconnaissance patrol of three men, he was ordered to get information about enemy positions in a thick wood that was known to be heavily mined. As he was advancing into the wood, a German position engaged him at close range with a pistol and grenades, wounding the sergeant with him. He silenced the post with machine gun fire and grenades, wounding two Germans and taking one prisoner, before resuming his patrol. As his citation records: 'His personal courage and coolness under fire enabled him to carry out a dangerous and difficult task whilst inflicting casualties on the enemy; the extent of his leadership and the manner in which he inspired his men can only be realised fully by talking to those he led.'

> " His personal courage and coolness under fire enabled him to carry out a dangerous and difficult task whilst inflicting casualties on the enemy; the extent of his leadership and the manner in which he inspired his men can only be realised fully by talking to those he led. "

A Royal Navy FRS.1 Sea Harrier comes in to land on HMS
Hermes at sunset in May 1982. The two aircraft carriers,
Hermes and Invincible, provided air cover for the South Atlantic
Task Force as well as aerial support for operations on the
Falklands themselves.

CAPTAIN ROBERT RYDER
VC

awarded 21 May 1942 • St Nazaire • Royal Navy

Robert Ryder was awarded one of five Victoria Crosses awarded for the daring raid launched against the Normandie Dock at St Nazaire. Ryder commanded the naval forces involved in this dramatic action that put the Normandie Dock beyond repair, preventing the German battleship *Tirpitz* from using it.

Robert Ryder was born in India, educated in England and joined the Royal Navy in 1926. By the beginning of the Second World War, Ryder was a lieutenant commander on board the battleship HMS *Warspite*. He went on to

command the frigate HMS *Fleetwood* for six months, before taking command of the infantry landing ship *Prince Philippe*, which was lost following a collision in thick fog in the Firth of Clyde. Without a ship, and confined to a desk

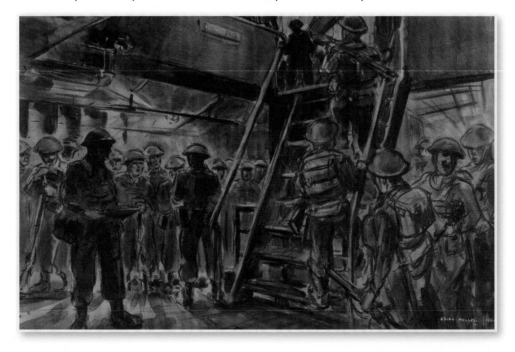

▶ Troops to Military Boat Stations, *by Brian Mullen. Commandos in full kit file on to deck for the tensest moment in a raid.*

job, he jumped at the chance to get involved in the Commando raid on St Nazaire.

The Normandie Dock at St Nazaire was the only dry dock on the Atlantic coast able to cope with the huge German battleship the *Tirpitz*, which was a serious threat to British transatlantic convoys. When the *Tirpitz* became operational in January 1942 a means had to be found to destroy the Normandie Dock, and an elaborate joint Naval and Commando operation was planned to carry this out. An old destroyer, HMS *Campbeltown*, escorted by a flotilla of motor launches, was to be packed full of explosives and rammed into the outer gate of the dry dock, while a team of Commandos demolished the dockside facilities.

On 26 March the flotilla set sail for St Nazaire, and on the night of 27/28 they made their way up the river Loire to the port and launched their attack on the port under heavy fire, with Ryder leading the way aboard a motor gun boat (MGB). The *Campbeltown* managed

to reach its target, ramming the outer gate of the dock, while the Commandos went ashore to carry out their demolition work. Ryder remained on board his MGB, giving covering fire all the way in an attempt to deal with the numerous German strongpoints around the harbour, while at the same time taking wounded crew from the other boats. Ryder and his crew remained under intense fire for over an hour until it was clear that they could do no more. By this time they were unable to evacuate the remaining Commandos and so withdrew, with the boat full of dead and wounded. The *Campbeltown* blew up later that morning, putting the dock out of operation for the remainder of the war.

Following the operation, Ryder also took part in the amphibious assault on the French port of Dieppe in 1942 and ended the war as a captain. He later served as a Conservative Member of Parliament from 1950 to 1955. Robert Ryder passed away in 1986.

▼ *The battered HMS Campbeltown stuck fast onto the outer gate of the Normandie Dock.*

GORDON BASTIAN

AM, MBE

awarded (AM) 17 August 1943 • Battle of the Atlantic • Merchant Navy

Gordon Bastian was awarded the Albert Medal, later exchanged for a George Cross in 1971, for saving the lives of two men when the ship on which he was second engineer officer was torpedoed by a German U-boat on the night of 30 March 1942.

▼ *An oil tanker explodes in the middle of the Atlantic.*

Born in South Wales, Gordon Bastian joined the Merchant Navy in the pre-war years and was in the forefront of the struggle against the German U-boats during the pivotal Battle of the Atlantic, the longest-running campaign of the Second World War.

At the outbreak of the war, the Admiralty had adopted the convoy system that had been so successful during the First World War, with the first trans-Atlantic convoy departing Halifax on 16 September 1939 to bring much-needed supplies to the British Isles. With the Fall of

France in the summer of 1940, the German U-boats moved to new bases along the French Atlantic coast, which made the crossing much more perilous.

By March 1942 Gordon Bastian had already received the MBE for his part in the Battle of the Atlantic, and he was second engineer officer aboard the SS *Empire Bowman*, which left Freetown in Sierra Leone bound for Liverpool as part of convoy SL 126. The convoy came under attack from U-boats, and the *Empire Bowman* was hit by a torpedo fired by *U-404*.

Bastian had been duty officer in the engine room and, realising that there were still two firemen on watch in the stokehold, he made his way through the water-filled darkness to rescue them. When the watertight door between the stokehold and the engine room was opened the men surged through in a rush of water, and

one of them had a broken arm and injured feet. Unable to help both at the same time, Bastian helped one of the men to the escape ladder before returning below to find the other man, during which time he was practically choked by cordite fumes. However, he managed to save the second man, and the *Empire Bowman*'s survivors were picked up by HMS *Wear* and taken to Liverpool.

Bastian was awarded the Albert Medal for his actions, exchanged for the GC in 1971, and the citation makes clear that the two firemen certainly owed their survival to 'his exceptional bravery, strength and presence of mind'. The damage to his lungs suffered by inhaling the cordite fumes ensured he would take no more part in the war and Bastian was invalided out of the Merchant Navy. He retired to Canada in 1947, and passed away in 1987.

▲ A Rescue Ship in the Atlantic, March 1943 *by George Plante. A rescue ship breaks away from the convoy to pick up survivors from a torpedoed ship.*

MEDICAL ASSISTANT KATE NESBITT
MC

awarded 11 September 2009 • Afghanistan • Royal Navy

▼ Soldiers of C Company, 1 Rifles, pictured on patrol during operations in the Nawa area of Helmand, Afghanistan. It was during this operation that Lance Corporal List was wounded and Medical Assistant Nesbitt earned the MC.

Kate Nesbitt, who was born in 1988, is the second woman to have been awarded the Military Cross and the first from the Royal Navy; indeed, she is the first member of the Royal Navy to have been awarded the MC since the Second World War. While serving as a medic with 3 Commando Brigade in Afghanistan, she saved the life of a soldier of 1st Battalion The Rifles who was wounded on patrol.

Kate Nesbitt was born in Plymouth to a military family; her father had been a colour sergeant in the Royal Marines, and she also had brothers serving in the armed forces. Having joined the Royal Navy in 2005, she trained as a Medical Assistant and was posted to Afghanistan from October 2008 to March 2009 as part of 3 Commando Brigade's deployment on Operation Herrick IX. She was attached to C Company, 1st Battalion The Rifles.

On 12 March 2009 the company was involved in a five-day operation in the Nawa region near Lashkar Gah, Helmand Province, designed to drive Taliban forces away from the region in the run-up to the Afghan presidential and provincial council elections due to be held in August 2009.

Whilst the company was engaged in handing out safety packs and food, and reassuring the local Afghan population, a Taliban force ambushed them and during the ensuing firefight a soldier from 1 Rifles, Lance Corporal John List, was shot through the neck. Hearing about the casualty over her radio, MA1 Nesbitt ran some 70 metres (230 feet) under fire over open ground before spending 45 minutes administering emergency first aid to List. She cleared his airways and stemmed the loss of blood, all the time under constant fire, as she sought to keep the badly wounded solider alive. As her citation clearly states: 'Nesbitt's actions throughout a series of offensive operations were exemplary; under fire and under pressure her commitment and courage were inspirational and made the difference between life and death. She performed in the finest traditions of her service.'

With the Taliban driven back, the area secured and the wounded soldier stabilised, a US Blackhawk helicopter came in and airlifted him to hospital.

▲ Medical Assistant Kate Nesbitt, the first woman in the Royal Navy to be awarded the MC, after being presented with her award by Prince Charles at Buckingham Palace on 27 November 2009.

▼ C Company, 1 Rifles, prepare to evacuate a casualty by helicopter following an engagement with Taliban fighters in the Nawa region.

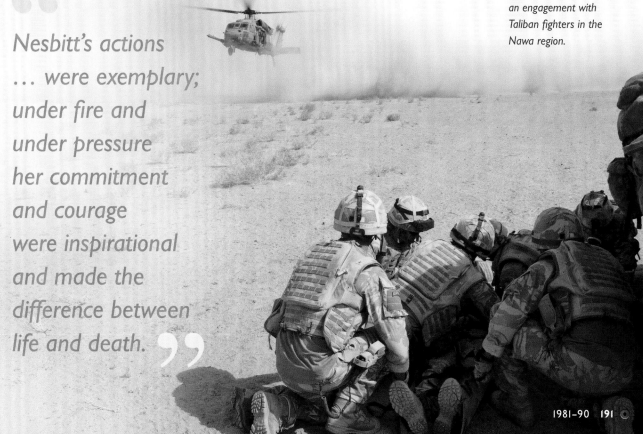

" Nesbitt's actions ... were exemplary; under fire and under pressure her commitment and courage were inspirational and made the difference between life and death. "

SQUADRON LEADER JAMES 'GINGER' LACEY
DFM AND BAR

awarded (DFM) 23 August 1940 • Battle of Britain • RAF

James 'Ginger' Lacey, who passed away in 1989, was the highest scoring Hurricane pilot over the course of the Battle of Britain, and the second top-scoring RAF pilot over the course of the Second World War.

▼ 'Ginger' Lacey boards a Supermarine Spitfire on 16 July 1941, having recently been promoted to flight lieutenant. He had just been presented with the first parachute manufactured in Australia, and a silk scarf autographed by the workers of the Sydney factory who made the parachute.

James Lacey was born and brought up in Wetherby, Yorkshire, and joined the RAF Reserve in 1937. At the outbreak of the Second World War he was called up to No. 501 Squadron as a sergeant pilot. No. 501 Squadron was committed to the battle for France in May 1940, and Lacey scored his first kills over Sedan on 13 May, shooting down a Messerschmitt Bf 109 and Bf 110. The squadron remained in France until 19 June, with Lacey having shot down two more German planes, and having crashed his plane into a swamp and nearly drowning.

The squadron was reorganised at RAF Croydon before fighting throughout the Battle of Britain as part of 11 Group, posted first to RAF Middle Wallop, then RAF Gravesend and finally RAF Kenley. It engaged the enemy on a record 35 days throughout the course of the battle, and it is therefore unsurprising that the squadron contained some notable aces, with Lacey the top scoring among them. Over the course of the Battle of Britain he shot down some 18 German aircraft, earning both the Distinguished Flying Medal and Bar, while at the same time he had been shot down or forced to land some nine times. On 15 September alone, later to be commemorated as Battle of Britain Day, Lacey shot down an He 111 and three Bf 109s, while also damaging another Bf 109.

Following the end of the Battle of Britain, Lacey remained with No. 501 Squadron when it converted to Spitfires in April 1941 and was promoted to flight lieutenant in July of that year. In August he was taken off combat operations and sent as an instructor to an operational training unit. He returned to front-line service in the Far East with No. 20 Squadron, before taking command of No. 155 Squadron in 1944 and No. 17 Squadron, with whom he won his last victory of the war when he shot down a Japanese Ki 43 'Oscar' over Burma on 19 February 1945. His final tally was 28 destroyed, five probably destroyed and nine damaged.

Squadron Leader Lacey, one of 'The Few', beside a Spitfire at RAF Henlow, Bedforshire, for the filming of Battle of Britain, *released in 1969.*

GENERAL SIR PETER DE LA BILLIÈRE

KCB, KBE, DSO, MC AND BAR, MSC

awarded (MC) 21 August 1959 • Oman and Borneo • 22nd SAS Regiment

▼ The cloth cap badge of the SAS. Designed by the regiment's first commanding officer, Colonel David Stirling, the winged dagger of the SAS and 'Who Dares Wins' motto have become famous worldwide.

Although perhaps most famous for his command of British forces during the first Gulf War of 1990/91, General Sir Peter de la Billière had a distinguished career as a junior officer with the 22nd Special Air Service Regiment (22 SAS), being awarded the Military Cross and Bar for his role in operations in Oman and Borneo in the 1950s and 1960s.

Peter de la Billière originally joined the King's Shropshire Light Infantry as a private in 1952, before being commissioned as a second lieutenant in the Durham Light Infantry (DLI). He served with the regiment on occupation duties in Japan, and on active service during the Korean War. In 1956 he managed to pass selection into the SAS and took command on active service, forging an association with the regiment that would last for much of his army career.

His first operational posting with the SAS was in Malaya, and following this he was sent to Oman, where he earned the first of his MCs. In mid-November

1958, D Squadron 22 SAS was deployed to the mountainous Jebel Akhdar region of Oman to take on the rebels that were based there, and Lieutenant de la Billière was awarded the MC for his role as a troop commander in charge of clearing enemy cave positions. Having returned to service with the DLI, and after a failure at Staff College, he returned to 22 SAS in 1964 as commander of A Squadron. This was a busy time for Special Forces and during his two years as a squadron commander, de la Billière served twice in Borneo during the Indonesian Confrontation, as well as in Saudi Arabia. He was awarded the Bar to his MC for his overall command, including leading his squadron on three highly successful missions that left a large number of the enemy dead.

Peter de la Billière later served as both second-in-command and commanding officer of 22 SAS, being responsible for the regiment

▲ *Lieutenant General Sir Peter de la Billière, left, with General Norman Schwarzkopf, at a press conference in late 1990. The command of British forces in the Middle East during the first Gulf War was the culmination of de la Billière's career.*

▶ *SAS Troopers descending into the jungle to complete the cordon during a search operation in Malay in 1953. Malay was to be Lieutenant Peter de la Billière's first operational deployment with 22 SAS.*

when it took part in another campaign in Oman, including the fabled battle of Mirbat. His final association with the regiment was as Director, Special Forces from 1978 to 1982, during which period the SAS rose to prominence for the successful conclusion of the Iranian Embassy siege in 1980.

CHAPTER EIGHT

1991–2000 Towards a new millennium

The in-depth review of the Legion undertaken at the end of the 1980s had profound effects on the way the organisation was run. By 1992, a new management board had been set up to control the day-to-day running of the Legion, streamlining decision-making and ensuring the Legion was more reactive to current events. A further degree of professionalism was brought to the Legion with the introduction of full-time County Field Officers (CFOs) to support the Legion's activity throughout the country. This was the most controversial part of the Legion's reforms, as the CFOs were paid directly out of money that could otherwise be used for benevolence. However, their introduction had a huge impact on local welfare and fundraising over the decade, and their expertise was much needed as the armed forces were going through a profound period of change

following the end of the Cold War. The 'options for change' introduced by the Government envisaged 64 000 servicemen and women leaving the army by 1995 alone, and these troops would be leaving the armed forces during a period of recession. The Legion, in conjunction with other organisations – such as the Soldiers' Sailors' and Airmens' Families Association – got involved in the process at a very early stage, helping in the planning with the Ministry of Defence and setting up a brand new training centre at Tidworth in Wiltshire, handily placed for many of the major army bases, which carried out a great deal of valuable work retraining servicemen and women. The Legion supported the armed forces in other ways as well: with so many deploying to the Gulf following Saddam Hussein's invasion of Kuwait, the Legion provided Christmas parcels to every single serviceman and servicewoman, as well as phone cards, sports equipment and other amenities. This proved so successful that in the following years they widened the scheme, sending parcels as far afield as Bosnia, Belize, Cambodia and the Falklands.

In addition to their active role in supporting the armed forces of the day, as well as those who had already served their country, the

▼ *Dame Vera Lynn (left) is joined by Elaine Paige (right) and Cliff Richard during the finale of the VE Day 50th anniversary Royal British Legion celebration concert in London's Hyde Park.*

1991	1992	1993	1994	1995
The Gulf War sees a large-scale deployment of British troops to the Middle East	Approval of new management structure for the Legion			The Legion takes centre stage in the VE Day anniversary celebrations in Hyde Park

Legion took a prominent role in events to commemorate the 50th anniversary of the Second World War, which occurred over the decade. In particular, the 50th anniversary of D-Day and the Battle for Normandy was a major highlight, with ceremonies taking place on the beaches themselves, while the great commemoration in Hyde Park on 8 May 1995, with the Queen in attendance, attracted considerable publicity for the Legion and its works.

The Legion's growing professionalism was reflected in the success of its appeals in the 1990s, with imaginative twists such as launching the Poppy Appeal in 1992 at El Alamein, with the sons of Montgomery and Rommel present, while the end of the decade saw the Legion's logo projected onto the canopy of the Millennium Dome in Greenwich.

These PR successes, coupled with a new approach to fundraising that focused more on keeping the momentum going throughout the year, rather than just around the time of the Poppy Appeal, saw an increasing amount of money going into the Legion's coffers. Modern management methods and techniques were introduced and plans laid for the 21st century.

There was considerable re-organisation to streamline efficiency and extend welfare services as well as laying the foundations for new and appropriate corporate governance.

Among many other successes was the Legion's campaign to reintroduce the two-minute silence at 11.00 a.m. on 11 November. This became an annual act, as it had been during the inter-war years. The Festival of Remembrance evolved to widen its audience and to highlight further the sacrifice of those who have served the country.

Another notable success was the campaign in 1999/2000 to achieve a gratuity (of £10,000 each) for former prisoners of war of the Japanese and their widows, which the Legion master-minded on behalf of the several membership organisations that make up the Far East Prisoner-of-War Association (FEPOW). It was a period of revitalisation, energy, drive and expansion in providing for the needs of ex-service people and their families in the new millennium.

▼Poppies bloom on Wellington Arch in London's Hyde Park to mark the 80th anniversary of The Royal British Legion's Poppy Appeal.

1996   **1997**   1998   1999   **2000**

Establishment of the National Memorial Arboretum in Staffordshire

The Legion takes a prominent role in the Millennium celebrations

MAJOR WILLIAM SIDNEY, FIRST VISCOUNT DE L'ISLE
VC, KG, GCMG, GCVO, KSTJ, PC

awarded (VC) 30 March 1944 • Anzio • Grenadier Guards

▼ *Three VC recipients pictured after receiving their medals from King George VI at Buckingham Palace on 10 October 1944. Left to right: Major William Sidney; Company Sergeant Major Stanley Hollis of the Green Howards; Brigadier Lorne Campbell.*

William Sidney, who died in 1991, was awarded his Victoria Cross as a temporary major in command of a company of the Grenadier Guards in the bitter fighting for the Anzio bridgehead in February 1944. He later had a distinguished career in both houses of parliament before serving as Governor General of Australia.

Born and raised in a privileged and aristocratic background, William Sidney was educated at Eton and Magdalene College, Cambridge, before joining the Grenadier Guards Reserve in 1929. He served with the Grenadier Guards throughout the Second World War. Sidney was awarded his VC for his actions in defence of the Anzio bridgehead on the night of 7/8 February 1944. The landings at Anzio were designed to bypass the formidable German defences of the Gustav Line, and two Allied divisions were put ashore on 22 January and the spent the following week consolidating the bridgehead.

The first major German counterattacks came on the night of 3/4 February, forcing the Allies back onto the defensive and at times nearly pushing them back into the sea. The fighting was particularly hard around the

200   1991–2000

towns of Aprilia and Caroceto, involving the 24th Guards Brigade, and it was here that Major William Sidney commanded the support company of the 5th Battalion the Grenadier Guards. On the night of 7/8 February, when he came under prolonged German infantry attack, Major Sidney personally led a series of charges armed with a Tommy gun and successfully drove the enemy back. Major Sidney sent the majority of his company back to get more ammunition while he held the line with two guardsmen. In the course of another German attack, a grenade killed one of the guardsmen and wounded both

Major Sidney and the other, leaving him to hold off the attacking Germans singlehandedly. He managed to hold them off until the ammunition party returned and he remained at his post until the fighting grew quieter and the Grenadiers' position had been consolidated.

Towards the end of the war he became the Conservative MP for Chelsea, and later took a seat in the House of Lords following the death of his father, serving as Secretary of State for Air under Winston Churchill from 1951 to 1955. He later served as Governor General of Australia from 1961 to 1965.

▼ *Men of the Cheshire Regiment in a captured German communications trench during the breakout offensive at Anzio, 22 May 1944.*

GROUP CAPTAIN GEOFFREY LEONARD CHESHIRE, BARON CHESHIRE

VC, OM, DSO AND TWO BARS, DFC

awarded (VC) 8 September 1944 • RAF

Leonard Cheshire, who passed away in 1992, was one of the most decorated RAF pilots of the Second World War. He was a successful bomber pilot, commander of the famous No. 617 Squadron, and the British observer of the atomic bomb dropped at Nagasaki on 9 August 1945.

▼ *Group Captain Cheshire's medal bar, with the VC on the far left.*

Born in Chester and educated in Oxford, Leonard Cheshire entered the RAF at the beginning of the Second World War and was posted to No. 102 Squadron, Bomber Command, flying Armstrong Whitworth Whitley medium bombers. He served in Bomber Command for the rest of his operational service, clocking up four tours of duty.

He earned his first award for valour, the Distinguished Service Order, on his first tour when his aircraft was struck by anti-aircraft attack and caught fire. Cheshire carried out his bombing raid regardless, before piloting his badly damaged aircraft back to base. Following the completion of his first tour he immediately volunteered for a second, this time with No. 35 Squadron on the

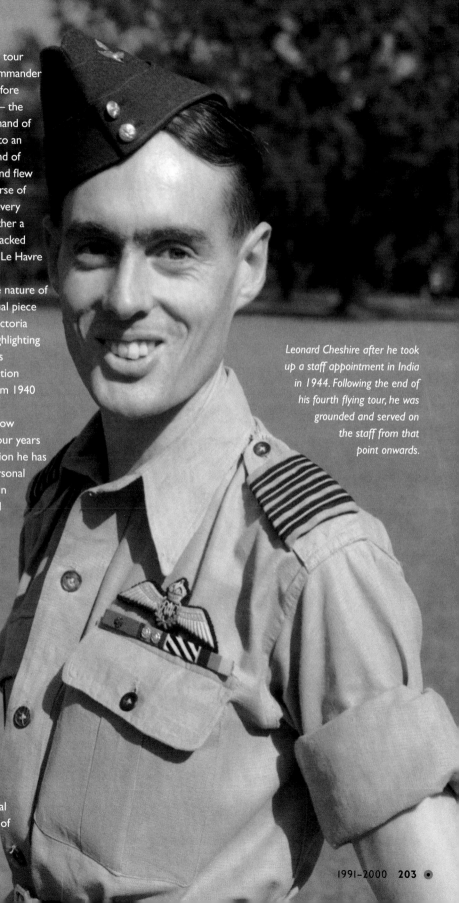

Handley Page Halifax. By the end of this tour he had been promoted to squadron commander and took charge of No. 76 Squadron before being promoted again to group captain – the youngest in the RAF – and taking command of RAF Marston Moor. Wanting to return to an operational flying role, he took command of No. 617 Squadron (the 'Dambusters'), and flew a fourth operational tour. Over the course of this tour, Cheshire led his squadron in every operation, directing their bombing in either a Mosquito or a P-51 Mustang as they attacked targets including the submarine pens at Le Havre and the V-weapon sites in Normandy.

Unusually, it was for the cumulative nature of his service rather than for one individual piece of gallantry that he was awarded the Victoria Cross in September 1944. Although highlighting particular missions, such as a hazardous one over Munich in April 1944, the citation emphasises his overall contribution from 1940 through to 1944:

'Wing Commander Cheshire has now completed a total of 100 missions. In four years of fighting against the bitterest opposition he has maintained a record of outstanding personal achievement, placing himself invariably in the forefront of the battle. What he did in the Munich operation was typical of the careful planning, brilliant execution and contempt for danger which has established for Wing Commander Cheshire a reputation second to none in Bomber Command.'

Following the completion of his fourth tour he served in staff positions for the rest of the war, although he served as Churchill's observer for the bombing of Nagasaki in August 1945.

After the end of the war he founded a community for ex-servicemen, which developed into the Leonard Cheshire Disability charity, an organisation that remains strong to this day. He was also heavily involved in the development of the World Memorial Fund, which in turn led to the creation of the National Memorial Arboretum.

Leonard Cheshire after he took up a staff appointment in India in 1944. Following the end of his fourth flying tour, he was grounded and served on the staff from that point onwards.

SERGEANT FRED KITE
MM AND TWO BARS

awarded (Bar to MM) 11 August 1944 • Northwest Europe • Royal Tank Regiment

▼ Sherman tanks carrying infantry wait for the order to advance at the start of Operation Goodwood on 18 July 1944.

Fred Kite, who died in 1993, was the only British soldier in the Second World War to be awarded two Bars to the Military Medal. Serving in North Africa, Crete, Greece and finally Normandy, he took part in some of the most famous British battles in the Second World War, and ended up one of the most decorated soldiers in the British Army.

Fred Kite joined 3rd Battalion the Royal Tank Regiment (3 RTR) on leaving school in Newcastle-under-Lyme, Staffordshire, at the age of 17 in 1939. This battalion saw an incredible amount of action in the Second World War. It was committed to the battle for France and was largely destroyed there, being re-formed and sent to Egypt, where it served in the Western Desert. The battalion was sent on the ill-fated expedition to Greece in March 1941, where it lost all of its armour. Re-formed again, it was part of 4th Armoured Brigade and took part in all the major battles of the war in the desert. It was here that Sergeant Kite earned his first MM, when he was involved in a reconnaissance operation near the Libyan town of Tarhuna in January 1943. Leading his troop forwards, he spotted the enemy anti-tank, machine-gun and artillery positions while exposed to their fire, allowing the British artillery to suppress them and 3 RTR to move on to its objective.

Towards the end of 1943, 3 RTR returned to England, where it began training to take part in the forthcoming battle for Normandy. As part of 11th Armoured Division, 3 RTR now took part in some of the most brutal fighting of the war as it battled the German armoured divisions in the various offensives around the city of Caen. Sergeant Kite was awarded two Bars to his MM for actions in this fighting. The first was on 18 and 19 July 1944 near the village of Bras, when he moved forwards to eliminate a German Panzer IV, Panther and 88mm anti-tank gun, allowing the rest of his squadron to move into better positions. The second and final action occurred on 3 August at Le Grand Bonfait when the troops he was supporting were counterattacked by a mixed infantry/armour German force. With all the nearby British tanks destroyed, Sergeant Kite carried on fighting at close range until his tank was finally disabled and he was seriously injured. However, his delaying action had proved enough, as his citation confirms: 'Sgt Kite showed the greatest personal courage and his example of remaining in action against all odds, that were much against him, was an inspiration to all. He undoubtedly helped to a considerable degree to beat off this attack on a feature of great importance.'

A British Crusader tank passes a burning German Pzkw Mk IV tank during Operation Crusader, November 1941.

" Sgt Kite showed the greatest personal courage and his example of remaining in action against all odds, that were much against him, was an inspiration to all. He undoubtedly helped to a considerable degree to beat off this attack on a feature of great importance. "

CAPTAIN CHARLES UPHAM
VC AND BAR

awarded (Bar to VC) 26 September 1945 • Crete and El Alamein • New Zealand Expeditionary Force

▼ *Second Lieutenant Charles Kazlett Upham (right) being congratulated by his platoon sergeant on the award of his first VC, 27 October 1941.*

Charles Upham, who died in 1994, was the only man to have been awarded the Victoria Cross and Bar in the Second World War, and the only combat soldier ever to do so. He fought in the Mediterranean throughout the war until his capture by the enemy at the Battle of El Alamein, after which he spent the rest of the war in prisoner of war camps, including the infamous Colditz Castle.

Born and raised in New Zealand, Charles Upham had served for five years in the Territorial Army and enlisted as a private in the New Zealand Expeditionary Force (NZEF) on the outbreak of the Second World War. Transported to the Middle East, Upham underwent officer training in Egypt and was a platoon commander at the time of the German invasion of Greece in 1941. Upham's battalion, among many others, was sent to Greece to attempt to stem the German advance. This was impossible, and the British forces withdrew to Crete, which was itself assaulted by a German airborne force in May 1941.

It was here that Upham earned the first of his two VCs. Over the course of nine days, from 22 to 30 May 1941, his platoon was in the forefront of the action. Upham distinguished himself in conducting numerous counterattacks. He single-handedly destroyed a number of German machine-gun posts near Maleme, rescued an injured man under fire, and, despite

being wounded several times, continued to lead his platoon in near-constant counter-attacks against the advancing Germans. Despite his heroics the British position on Crete could not be held, and he and his men were evacuated to Egypt. There, he was promoted to captain and placed in command of a company.

Upham was awarded the Bar to the VC at the First Battle of El Alamein in July 1942. The New Zealand Division was tasked with capturing the vital Ruweisat Ridge, one of the cornerstones of the Alamein position, and Upham's battalion was part of the attack. While reconnoitring the position, Upham was twice wounded and at the same time managed to destroy a truckload of German infantry. However, he still led his men forward in the night attack, being wounded once more when a bullet shattered his elbow. Despite this, he carried on leading his men until the position was captured, before having his wounds attended to. He returned to his company in time to face heavy German counter-attacks, until, having been wounded again and with his company reduced to six men, his position was overrun and he was captured.

Having recovered from his wounds in an Italian hospital, he attempted to escape several times and was sent to Colditz Castle, where he remained for the rest of the war.

CORPORAL WAYNE MILLS
CGC

awarded 9 May 1995 • Bosnia • Duke of Wellington's Regiment (West Riding)

▼ *A Yugoslavian-manufactured PMR 3 anti-personnel fragmentation stake mine. This example comes from the war in Kosovo in 1999, but these weapons proliferated throughout the whole region.*

Wayne Mills was the first recipient of the Conspicuous Gallantry Cross, a new award instituted in 1993 and second only to the Victoria and George Crosses. Corporal Mills was awarded the CGM for actions during his deployment as part of Great Britain's commitment to the UN Protection Force in Bosnia-Herzegovina in 1994.

British forces had become involved in the war in Bosnia in 1992, when a force based around the 1st Battalion The Cheshire Regiment was sent to the country under the codename Operation Grapple. The situation in Bosnia had gradually deteriorated. While fighting had been going on in Croatia since 1991, fighting had finally broken out at roughly the same time as Bosnia declared its independence following a referendum in March 1992. The UN Protection Force (UNPROFOR) had already been formed, initially for deployment in Croatia, to act as a mediator between the warring sides and to escort aid convoys in the conflict zone, and its mandate was extended to the new conflagration in Bosnia.

It was here that Corporal Mills earned the CGC in 1994. This was a new award and had been instituted only in 1993, when the British Army conducted a review of the honours system. The previous system had been based on rank, with certain medals available only for officers, while NCOs and private soldiers were eligible for others.

The new CGC was designed to replace the Distinguished Conduct Medal (Army) and the Conspicuous Gallantry Medal (Air and Naval) as awards for other ranks, and the Distinguished Service Order as an award for officers. At the same time, the Military Cross was made accessible to all ranks, and the Military Medal was discontinued.

Corporal Mills received his award for his actions on a patrol in Bosnia on 29 April 1994. Mills was leading the patrol when it came under small-arms fire from a group of Bosnian Serbs. Mills's patrol returned fire, killing a number of the attackers, and began to withdraw towards their base with the Serbian force following them as they did so. When the British patrol reached an open clearing, leaving themselves highly vulnerable to attack, Corporal Mills turned back and engaged the Serbian forces, allowing his men to cross the clearing unscathed. During the ensuing firefight Corporal Mills shot the leader of the Serbian group and forced the rest to scatter, and then managed to return to his patrol.

◀ Colour Sergeant Wayne Mills CGC, 1st Battalion The Duke of Wellington's Regiment (West Riding).

▼ A Warrior IFV used by Colonel Bob Stewart, commander of 1st Battalion The Cheshire Regiment, makes its way over an unsafe bridge in Bosnia. The Warrior is painted in the high visibility white colour scheme identifying UNPROFOR vehicles.

An RAF Tornado F3 in flight over burning oil wells in Kuwait, January 1991.
Following Saddam Hussein's invasion of Kuwait in August 1990 a major
coalition aerial campaign, launched on 17 January 1991, served to degrade
the Iraqi forces prior to the start of ground operations on 23 February 1991.

CORPORAL BRYAN BUDD
VC

awarded 14 December 2006 • Afghanistan • Parachute Regiment

Bryan Budd of 3rd Battalion The Parachute Regiment (3 Para),
who joined the army in 1996, was awarded the Victoria Cross
posthumously for his repeated bravery in fighting around the town of
Sangin in Helmand Province, Afghanistan, during July and August 2006.
He remains the only soldier to have been awarded the highest award
for bravery during the ongoing war in Afghanistan.

▼ *Corporal Bryan Budd,
3 Para, shown during his
tour of Afghanistan.*

Corporal Budd was originally from Belfast in
Northern Ireland and joined the British Army
in 1996. He had served for many years in the
Parachute Regiment's elite Pathfinder Platoon.
At the time of his deployment to Afghanistan, he
was posted to A Company, 3 Para, based in the
town on Sangin in Helmand Province. The year
2006 was the first in which British troops had
deployed to Helmand Province in any significant
numbers, and the scale of the fighting was a
shock to many involved. The heart of the British
deployment was 3 Para, and it was this unit that
saw much of the fighting in and around Sangin
District Centre, one of the most troubled spots
in the summer of 2006.

It was here that, on 27 July, Bryan Budd
carried out the first of a series of acts that
would lead to the award of the VC. While on a
routine patrol his section came under fire from
a nearby rooftop and two of his men were hit,
one seriously. Taking the initiative, Corporal
Budd immediately led an attack on the building

◀ British soldiers from 3 Para and 1 Royal Irish conduct clearance patrols in and around the town of Sangin, Helmand Province, Afghanistan. Sangin saw some of the fiercest clashes between British Forces and Taliban Insurgents during Operation Herrick IV.

▼ A member of A Company, 3 Para, watches over the Company base in Sangin. The Para bases in Sangin came under constant small-arms, mortar and rocket-propelled grenade (RPG) attack while they were based there over the summer of 2006.

containing the gunmen, forcing them to abandon their positions and giving the necessary time to evacuate the wounded.

A month later Corporal Budd was again on patrol when he became involved in the incident that was to cost him his life. While attempting to outflank a force of Taliban, his section was spotted and came under heavy fire. Three of his men were wounded and the section was pinned down. Realising that, if the situation remained as it was, there was every chance that more of his men would be wounded or even killed, Corporal Budd charged across a cornfield towards the Taliban position. Despite being wounded, he reached the Taliban position and either killed them or forced them to flee, thus allowing time for the remaining men in his section to regroup. Following a concerted effort to recover his body, it was found surrounded by three dead Taliban. His determination and inspiration are credited in his citation (see right).

> " His determination to press home a single-handed assault against a superior enemy force despite his wounds stands out as a premeditated act of inspirational leadership and supreme valour. "

DAME KELLY HOLMES

DBE, MBE

awarded (DBE) 31 December 2004 • athlete, mentor and fund-raiser

▼ Kelly Holmes launching the Poppy Appeal with Colin Antink in 2004. Colin, whose father was a paratrooper, suffers from a rare degenerative injury and the Legion has supported his education.

Dame Kelly Holmes is most famous for her stunning gold-medal victories in the 800m and 1500m at the 2004 Athens Olympics. However, she also spent nine-and-a-half years in the British Army, before leaving in 1997, and has supported the British Legion in its activities, helping to launch the Poppy Appeal in 2004.

◀ The moment Kelly Holmes won the 1500m gold medal at the Athens Olympics in 2004.

Kelly was born and raised in Kent and became interested in athletics while at school, having been encouraged by her PE teacher. Joining Tonbridge Athletics Club at the age of 12, she teamed up with coach Dave Arnold, who was to prove extremely influential on her early athletic career.

In 1988 she gave up athletics and joined the British Army, initially serving as an HGV driver in the Women's Royal Army Corps. While in the Army she retrained as a physical training instructor (PTI), qualifying in 1991. The Army encouraged Kelly in her sporting enthusiasm, and she became Army Judo champion as well as representing the Army at volleyball.

Following the Barcelona Olympics in 1992, Kelly decided to get involved in Athletics again seriously. She ran at the World Championships in Stuttgart in 1993, breaking the English world record for the 800m. From this point onwards she realised that she had a serious chance of competing for major honour. For the next four years she combined her athletic training while serving as a soldier, being promoted to the rank of sergeant, before she decided in 1997 to leave the Army and commit to full-time training.

Kelly was dogged by a series of injuries throughout her athletic career, the most serious of which was a ruptured calf and torn Achilles tendon at the World Championships in Athens in 1997, an injury from which she took nearly a year to recover. She bounced back to win silver in the Commonwealth games in 1998 and then a bronze medal in the 800m at the Sydney Olympics in 2000.

Having trained extensively in South Africa during the early 2000s, and winning five more major championship medals, Kelly entered the run-up to the Athens Olympics of 2004 with no injury worries and in the best shape of her life. This good form led to staggering results when Kelly won the 800m final on 23 August 2004, the first British woman to win a track-and-field event since Sally Gunnell in 1992. She followed this by winning the 1500m final on 28 August, breaking the British record in the process. Kelly was the winner of the BBC Sports Personality of the Year in 2004 and was made a Dame Commander of the Order of the British Empire in the 2005 New Year's Honours List; she had already been awarded the MBE in 1998 for her Army service.

Since her retirement from Athletics in 2005, Kelly has been deeply involved both in mentoring young middle-distance athletes, and in charity work, setting up her own organisation, the DKH Legacy Trust (www.doublegold.co.uk), to support and inspire young people. Among the many charities she works with is the Royal British Legion, for which she has a strong affection given her military background. She helped to launch the Poppy Appeal in 2004 and has been involved with the Legion ever since.

GENERAL SIR MICHAEL JACKSON
GCB, CBE, DSO AND BAR, DL

awarded (DSO) 28 October 1999 • Kosovo • Parachute Regiment

General Sir Mike Jackson, who was knighted in 1998, commanded the NATO forces sent into Kosovo in 1999 before going on to serve as Chief of the General Staff, the highest position in the British Army.

▶ *Paratroopers of the 1st Battalion The Parachute Regiment prepare to embark on RAF Puma helicopters as they move forward to Pristina, the capital of Kosovo, on 12 June 1999.*

◀ *General Sir Mike Jackson arriving at Westminster Abbey for the National Service of Remembrance and Commemoration of the 60th anniversary of the end of the Second World War, 10 July 2005, as part of Veteran's Awareness Week.*

Born into a military family, Jackson went into the army straight from school, entering Sandhurst in 1962. Following his graduation he joined the Intelligence Corps and undertook a degree in Russian Studies at the University of Birmingham. Jackson remained in the Intelligence Corps until 1970, at which point he transferred into the Parachute Regiment. He was present with 1st Battalion The Parachute Regiment at Bloody Sunday on 30 January 1972, and with 2nd Battalion The Parachute Regiment at the Warrenpoint Massacre on 27 August 1979.

Jackson went on to command 1 Para from 1984 to 1986, before commanding 39 Infantry Brigade. Promoted to major general in May 1992, he took command of the 3rd Mechanised Division which later formed the basis of the NATO Multinational Division South-West, part of the NATO-led Implementation Force on the ground in Bosnia. Jackson was then appointed to command NATO's Allied Rapid Reaction Corps (ARRC) and promoted to lieutenant general in January 1997. This force served in Bosnia in the late 1990s and was committed to Kosovo following NATO operations there in 1999.

Widespread violence erupted in 1998 in Kosovo as the predominantly Serb police and military authorities cracked down on the local Albanian population, and fought openly with the irregular Kosovo Liberation Army. Faced with the threat of ethnic cleansing, NATO intervened militarily between March and June 1999, with an air campaign that included attacks on Belgrade. A peace agreement was signed on 10 June 1999, which led to Operation Joint Guardian, the deployment of the NATO rapid reaction force under the command of Lieutenant General Jackson, during which he managed to deal successfully with an uneasy stand-off between NATO and Russian forces at Pristina Airport. For his command of this force in Kosovo, he received the Distinguished Service Order on 28 October 1999.

Following his return to the UK in 2000, Jackson was promoted to full general and became Chief of the General Staff, the highest position in the British Army, in 2003 just prior to the invasion of Iraq. Having served in this role for three years, General Sir Mike Jackson retired from the army in 2006.

WARRANT OFFICER CLASS 2 KARL LEY

GM

awarded 24 September 2010 • Afghanistan • Royal Logistics Corps

▼ Soldiers from A Company, 4 Rifles, in Sangin march in single file along a route being cleared by a Vallon operator.

Karl 'Badger' Ley deactivated 139 explosive devices during one tour of operations in Afghanistan, more than twice as many as any other bomb disposal expert, and was awarded the George Medal for his skill and bravery.

Karl Ley was born and raised in Sheffield and joined the army in 1999, going into the Royal Logistic Corps (RLC). He trained as an ammunition technician – responsible for all aspects of ammunition and explosives handling, including defusing bombs and improvised explosive devices (IEDs) – and was posted to 11 Explosive Ordnance Disposal (EOD) Regiment. In ten years with the army he served in the Falklands, Northern Ireland, Iraq and Belize, before deploying to Afghanistan in September 2009.

A staff sergeant at the time, Karl Ley commanded an IED Detection team of four men, part of the Counter-IED (CIED) Task Force based in Helmand Province to deal with the ever-present threat of Taliban IEDs faced by British troops in the region. As a 'high threat'

▲ *Staff Sergeant Karl 'Badger' Ley at the end of his six-month tour, in which he defused 139 bombs.*

> *Ley has worked tirelessly in the most hazardous of conditions, enduring both mental and physical fatigue. He has sadly lost seven of his colleagues, including three close friends, within the Counter-IED Task Force but he has continued undaunted. For this unwavering dedication, conspicuous gallantry and poise in the face of substantial danger and of the enemy, over a sustained period, he is unreservedly recommended for high public recognition.*

operator, Ley was trained to deal with the most complex and dangerous of Taliban devices, and his six-month tour gave him plenty of opportunity to put his skills into practice. Not only did he managed to deactivate a staggering 139 devices over the course of his tour, but 28 of these were in one location over a 72-hour period of intense activity, with 14 defused over nine hours. All of this took place under Taliban fire and in extreme physical conditions, with the IED disposal teams (IEDD) unable to wear their heavy protective equipment owing to the extreme heat.

This was an extremely testing period for the CIED Task Force, as they were in the forefront of Operation Moshtarak, a major International Security Assistance Force (ISAF) effort to pacify large areas of Helmand province, launched in February 2010. The IEDD teams were on constant call to clear the avenues of advance for the ISAF forces, and they suffered significant casualties, including the tragic death of Staff Sergeant Olaf Schmid, a close personal friend of Karl Ley, at the end of October.

Karl Ley's citation makes clear the difficulties of his job and the reasons he was awarded a well-deserved GM: 'Ley has worked tirelessly in the most hazardous of conditions, enduring both mental and physical fatigue. He has sadly lost seven of his colleagues, including three close friends, within the Counter-IED Task Force but he has continued undaunted. For this unwavering dedication, conspicuous gallantry and poise in the face of substantial danger and of the enemy, over a sustained period, he is unreservedly recommended for high public recognition.'

MAJOR PHIL ASHBY
QGM

awarded 6 April 2001 • Sierra Leone • Royal Marines

Major Phil Ashby was awarded the Queen's Gallantry Medal for his dramatic escape from rebel-held territory in war-torn Sierra Leone. When the United Nations (UN) peacekeeping mission he was engaged on went wrong, he trekked for nearly a week through hostile jungle, leading three other officers to eventual safety.

▼ *Three soldiers from 1 Parachute Regiment confer under the regimental flag during Operation Palliser.*

Phil Ashby was commissioned in the Royal Marines at the age of 17, making him the youngest officer in the forces, and he went on to become the youngest major at the age of 28. Having served with the Marines as a mountain leader and jungle-warfare instructor, as well as commanding troops in such varied locations as Norway, Brunei and Belize, he volunteered to serve in Sierra Leone as a UN peacekeeper in January 2000, with the role of disarming the rebel fighters of the Revolutionary United Front (RUF).

Sierra Leone has had a turbulent history since its independence in 1961, with democratic rule being punctuated by periods of civil war and anarchy – largely driven by the vast reserves of mineral wealth in the country. The RUF had been formed in neighbouring Liberia in the late 1980s and had been conducting a guerrilla campaign since the early 1990s. There had been progress towards a peace deal in 1999 and UN troops had been brought into the country, the United Nations Mission in Sierra Leone (UNAMSIL), to help bring about disarmament of the various armed factions. However, the RUF still remained largely in opposition to the process, harassing the UN and undermining their operations.

◀ UN monitors stand together after escaping from Sierra Leone RUF rebels. Left to right: British Major Phil Ashby, British Major Andrew Samsonoff, New Zealander Major David Lingard, and British Lieutenant Paul Rowland.

It was in this atmosphere that Major Ashby arrived in the country, and he and other UN workers found themselves caught up in the situation in May 2000. Trapped in a small compound surrounded by rebels, they endured four days of siege before they realised that they had to make their own way out. Going over the wall of the compound the following morning, Major Ashby and the three other officers who accompanied him trekked for nearly a week through remote jungle, surrounded by hostile forces and short of both food and water. Eventually they reached safety in the form of a UN contingent from Guinea, following which they were airlifted back to the capital Freetown.

In May 2000 the situation in Sierra Leone had deteriorated, and the capital, Freetown, was under clear threat from the rebel RUF forces. The situation led to the deployment of the 1st Battalion The Parachute Regiment, along with supporting forces, to facilitate the evacuation of British nationals. The role of this force expanded into more general support of the government and UN forces and they provided an important factor in the stabilisation of the situation and its eventual peaceful outcome.

Royal Air Force and Royal Navy helicopters operating at Lungi Airport at Freetown during Operation Palliser. A RAF HC2 Chinook from No. 7 Squadron RAF Odiham prepares to take off as a Royal Navy Sea King flies past.

CHAPTER NINE

90 years of service

The last decade has seen the British armed forces stretched to the very limit. The war in Iraq from 2003, in addition to the commitment to Afghanistan – originally quite small in 2001 but dramatically increased from 2006 onwards – have seen the British Army in particular be engaged in some its toughest fighting since the Second World War, and it has suffered a high level of casualties in the process.

These conflicts, along with their other operational deployments, have placed more stress on the armed forces than at any other point in the post-war period. The reduced number of personnel has meant that operational tours became more and more common as the years passed, with servicemen and servicewomen on a constant cycle of deployment. This has placed an inevitable pressure on those deployed, as well as on those left at home, and the Legion has played a vital role in supporting the armed forces politically, as well as helping those damaged in the conflicts, and maintaining its duty of care to all those veterans of the 20th century still requiring their aid.

In September 2007 the Legion launched the 'Honour the Covenant' campaign, calling on the Government to honour its commitment to the military covenant, the implicit agreement between the armed forces and the Government. The Legion also supported the right of Gurkha soldiers to remain in the UK at the end of their term of service – a claim that the High Court found was justified and part of the same military covenant.

In the light of the many life-changing injuries suffered by military personnel in both Iraq and Afghanistan, the Legion has also campaigned for changes to the Armed Forces Compensation Scheme, highlighting the injustices done to those who have suffered for their country and require long-term care. This campaign has proved successful and the sums available have now been increased. And further to its campaigning role, the Legion has also taken practical measures, providing financial help to over 10 000 veterans of Iraq and Afghanistan since 2003. It has also invested £50 million in Personnel Recovery Centres and the Battle Back Centre to care for the wounded of current conflicts. This is not to mention the day-to-day routine help and support it gives out to ex-servicemen and ex-servicewomen

▼ *An array of lapel poppies.*

2001   2002   2003   2004   2005

Launch of Operation Enduring Freedom and the first commitment of British forces in Afghanistan

US and Allied forces launch the invasion of Iraq, leading to a long-term British deployment

IT ONLY TAKES
A SECOND
TO PUT ON
A POPPY.

SHOULDER TO SHOULDER WITH ALL WHO SERVE

THE ROYAL BRITISH
LEGION

To donate text POPPY to 70090*
08458 395 717 www.poppy.org.uk
*Cost £5 Plus standard network charges (at least £4 goes to the Poppy Appeal) info@britishlegion.org.uk Reg. Charity No. 219279

through services such as Legionline, its direct telephone service.

As of 2010, the Legion spent £114 million in total on its benevolent work, with its fundraising activities raising £115.2 million – including a record £35 million for the Poppy Appeal. The rest came from a mixture of donations, funds from legacies, sponsorship, corporate support and fundraising events.

With its profile never higher thanks to its prominent campaigning on behalf of the ex-service community, and its fundraising invigorated by a range of innovative techniques, the Legion enters its tenth decade well placed to carry on its fine tradition of support and care. Although there are no veterans of the First World War left, and the numbers of veterans of the Second World War are dwindling, there are still more than 9 million people in the UK eligible to call on the Legion for support, and it remains willing and able to answer their call.

▲ *A Poppy Appeal poster from 2010. The Appeal still provides the largest share of the Legion's income, and the 2010 one was the most successful ever.*

▼ *Veterans, Legion officials and cadets attend a wreath-laying ceremony at Ranville Cemetery, Normandy, on 5 June 2009.*

2006   2007   2008   2010   2011

(2003–2007) The Legion launches the 'Honour the Covenant' campaign in support of the armed forces

The Poppy Appeal is the most successful ever, with £35 million raised

90th anniversary of the foundation of the Royal British Legion and the Poppy Appeal

AIR VICE MARSHAL JAMES EDGAR 'JOHNNIE' JOHNSON

CB, CBE, DSO AND TWO BARS, DFC AND BAR

awarded (DFC) 30 September 1941 • Northwest Europe • RAF

▼ 'Johnnie' Johnson on 6 July 2000 at Duxford Imperial Air Museum, Cambridgeshire, with a Spitfire Mk XIV painted with his initials to represent his own aircraft from the war. Johnson was the highest-scoring Allied fighter pilot, with 38 'kills'.

'Johnnie' Johnson, who passed away in 2001, was the highest-scoring Allied pilot in Northwest Europe, shooting down at least 38 German aircraft over Great Britain and occupied Europe in the course of the Second World War. He received many honours for his achievements, including the Distinguished Service Order and two Bars, and the Distinguished Flying Cross and Bar.

Johnson's record is all the more impressive considering that he was rejected by the RAF at his first attempt, before the outbreak of war. A collarbone injury caused by playing rugby was the reason for his rejection, but he joined the Leicestershire Yeomanry instead. A second attempt to join the RAFVR following the outbreak of the war was successful, although he still required an operation on his troublesome collarbone before he could begin operational flying, which meant he missed both the Battle of France and the Battle of Britain.

Once he was finally fit to resume flying in 1941 he served with No. 616 Squadron, part of the famous Tangmere Wing commanded by Douglas Bader. Johnson quickly proved his ability and was awarded his first DFC in September 1941, having taken part in 46 sorties and shot down four enemy aircraft. His Bar followed on 26 June 1942, with the citation calling him an 'excellent leader'. It was these leadership skills that were to come to the fore when he took command of No. 610 Squadron, taking part in closely fought fighter action over the Allied assault on the French port of Dieppe. In March 1943, as an acting wing commander, he took over the Canadian Wing, which became one of the highest-scoring RAF fighter wings. While carrying out fighter sweeps over occupied France or escorting USAAF bomber formations, Johnson steadily increased his tally of victories, and he was awarded the first of his three DSOs on June 1943, with the second following in September of the same year.

Placed in charge of another Canadian unit, 144 Wing, he led them over the Normandy beaches before they became the first fighter wing to be based on the Continent. Johnson carried on flying operationally right through to the end of the war, and, until his retirement in 1966, he served in the RAF as an air vice marshal and AOC Air Forces Middle East.

MARINE
BILL SPARKS
DSM

awarded 29 June 1943 • Operation Frankton • Royal Marines

▼ Bill Sparks, the last of the Cockleshell Heroes, on the River Thames, where he attended the launch of the British Legion Poppy Appeal.

Bill Sparks, who died in 2002, was the last surviving member of the 'Cockleshell Heroes', the daring commandos who launched a canoe-born attack on the German-occupied port of Bordeaux in December 1942.

● **228** 2001–2011

◀ Major 'Blondie' Haslar, commander of the Royal Marine Boom Patrol Detachment during Operation Frankton. Haslar commanded the BPD in the Aegean before going to the Far East as second-in-command of the Small Operations Group.

▶ HMS Tuna, with her Jolly Roger flying after success against a U-boat, approaches the depot ship HMS Forth at Holy Loch, 26 August 1943. The Tuna was the submarine that transported the Royal Marine Boom Patrol Detachment to the mouth of the Gironde on 7 December 1942.

Born in the East End of London, Bill Sparks volunteered for the Royal Marines and signed up for special duties following the death of his brother when his ship HMS Naiad was sunk by a U-boat in the Mediterranean in March 1942.

The special duties Bill Spark signed up for turned out to be membership of the Royal Marine Boom Patrol Detachment, a unit founded by Major H. G. Haslar – a Royal Marine officer serving with Combined Operations – to target enemy shipping using small craft, particularly canoes, and explosives.

The most famous of the unit's exploits was Operation Frankton, an assault on merchant shipping in Bordeaux Harbour. On 7 December 1942 ten men in five canoes launched from the submarine HMS Tuna for the raid and travelled 90 miles (145km) up the Gironde River to the port of Bordeaux. Bill Sparks shared a canoe with his commanding officer, Major Haslar.

Despite the loss of three of the canoes on the journey, Sparks and Haslar and the other remaining canoe team managed to reach Bordeaux on the night of 10/11 December. The following evening they placed their limpet mines on the merchant shipping before scuttling their canoes down river and setting off overland in an attempt to make their way to safety.

The mines exploded on the morning of the 12th, with 13 explosions seriously damaging five of the merchant vessels. The Royal Marines, however, had paid a very heavy price for their success. In the course of reaching Bordeaux, two canoes were lost and a further one damaged, two men were drowned, and, out of

the surviving marines, only Haslar and Sparks managed to escape German capture and make their way to the Spanish border. The other six men were taken prisoner and shot by the Germans.

Bill Sparks was awarded the Distinguished Service Medal for his role in the operation and continued to serve with the Royal Marines in Burma, Africa and Italy.

Following the end of the war he became a trolley-bus driver with London Transport, while also spending a year in Malaya during the Emergency in 1952.

This legend in Royal Marines history passed away in 2002, having been deeply involved in the commemoration of the exploits of the Cockleshell Heroes for the last years of his life.

LANCE CORPORAL JUSTIN THOMAS
CGC

awarded 31 October 2003 • Iraq • Royal Marines

Justin Thomas was awarded the Conspicuous Gallantry Cross for his actions during an Iraqi ambush in the early days of Operation Telic, the Allied invasion of Iraq. Under heavy fire he manned an exposed machine gun on a soft-skin vehicle and allowed his comrades to re-group before launching a successful counter-attack.

▼ Royal Marines of 40 Commando are landed ashore on the Al Faw Peninsula by Royal Air Force Chinook HC2 helicopters.

Born in Wales, Justin Thomas joined the Royal Marines at the age of 19 and was a lance corporal in charge of a machine-gun section of the Manoeuvre Support Group of 40 Commando, a heavily armed unit supporting the rifle companies of the Commando. 40 Commando was involved right from the start of

the invasion of Iraq, and Thomas and his section were airlifted by Chinook helicopter onto the Al Faw Peninsula on the night of 19/20 March 2003 in order to prevent the destruction of the oil terminals there and open up the approaches to the port of Um Qasr and the major city of Basra beyond.

By 30 March, 40 Commando had spent ten days fighting and patrolling through the Al Faw Peninsula and had reached the outer suburbs of the city of Basra. At this point a major operation, codenamed Operation James, was launched to clear the suburb of Abu al Khasib. The whole of 40 Commando, supported by engineers and armoured units from the Queen's Dragoon Guards, was in the line, with the Manoeuvre Support Group tasked with securing a key junction on the western flank.

Lance Corporal Thomas and his men had advanced throughout the day, coming under fire from all directions, until they found themselves under a heavy mortar bombardment, rapidly followed up by a salvo of anti-tank rockets. The marines had abandoned

◄ *Royal Marine Lance Corporal Justin Thomas holds his CGC after being decorated by Queen Elizabeth II at an investiture for services in Iraq at Buckingham Palace, 25 February 2004.*

their exposed 4 x 4 Pinzgauer vehicles and taken cover, but were now being pinned down by the heavy fire. It was only a matter of time before they began to take casualties. Realising this, Lance Corporal Thomas ran to one of the exposed vehicles and opened fire on the enemy positions with the vehicle mounted GPMG, keeping up a steady rate of fire while the other members of his troop re-formed and began to engage the enemy. Having regained the initiative, and with the support of artillery and air strikes, the marines subdued the Iraqi position and were able to resume the advance. His exceptional courage and leadership in the face of a well-armed and determined enemy was outstanding.

▼ *Members of 40 Commando, Royal Marines survey the wreckage of an Iraqi T54/55 tank on the outskirts of Basra.*

CORPORAL OF HORSE GLYNN BELL
MC

awarded 23 April 2004 • Iraq • Blues and Royals

Glynn Bell was serving with the Blues and Royals in Iraq in the aftermath of the invasion of 2003 when his unit was called upon to assist in extricating men of the Parachute Regiment who were trapped in a nearby town. Exposing his vehicle to heavy fire, Bell was crucial in ensuring that the trapped troops escaped to safety.

▼ Men of the Household Cavalry Regiment take fuel, water and food on board a Scimitar tank in Southern Iraq. It was an armoured vehicle like this that would take the brunt of the Iraqi firepower during the mission to extract the trapped British troops in Al Majar Al Kabir.

Corporal of Horse Glynn Bell was a long-service NCO when he was deployed to Kuwait in 2003 with the Blues and Royals. His squadron was deployed in a formation reconnaissance role for the 16th Air Assault Brigade. The invasion saw them suffer casualties from a friendly fire incident, and also as the result of an accident, but they saw very little in terms of action against the enemy. Following the invasion itself, the British forces in the south of Iraq became engaged in more of a peacekeeping operation. Despite the apparent calm there were still challenges, and on 24 June 2003 a platoon of 1st Battalion the Parachute Regiment, which had been searching for weapons in the nearby town of Al Majar Al Kabir, had come under attack and been forced into buildings, with their vehicles destroyed and their positions surrounded.

Glynn Bell's troop of Scimitar armoured vehicles was ordered forward as part of a quick reaction force to help extract the Paras from their perilous position. The armoured vehicles came under sustained fire as soon as they entered the town, with the threat of rocket propelled grenades (RPGs) ever present. Although the Scimitar was armoured, it would not withstand a direct hit from an RPG.

Finally locating the first batch of beleaguered Paras, Corporal of Horse Bell pushed his vehicle forward into an exposed position in order to draw the Iraqi fire and allow the Paras time to be resupplied wit tion and to get out of their position. They repeated this when they came to further trapped Paras and, with the decks of their vehicles loaded with men, withdrew back to their base at Al Amarah. The citation for Glynn Bell (below) emphasises his role in the operation.

> *Throughout the action, he displayed enormous courage. His leadership was, on its own, worthy of merit. His courage and tenacity under fire was central to the safe extraction of the platoon.*

▲ *Members of the 1st Battalion The Royal Green Jackets await the landing of their helicopter transport in Iraq in October 2003.*

▼ *The more traditional side of the Household cavalry. Guards of the Blues and Royals approaching Horseguards on a wintry January morning in London.*

LANCE CORPORAL JOHNSON BEHARRY VC

awarded 18 March 2005 • Iraq • Princess of Wales's Royal Regiment

Lance Corporal Beharry became the first person to be awarded the Victoria Cross since the Falklands War of 1982. He was awarded the highest award for valour in the face of the enemy for his bravery in twice saving members of his unit from ambush in Iraq in May and June 1994.

Originally born and brought up on the Caribbean island of Grenada, Johnson Beharry moved to the UK in 1999 and joined the army in 2001, serving in 1st Battalion The Princess of Wales's Royal Regiment. He served as the driver of a Warrior IFV with the battalion's C Company in Kosovo and Northern Ireland before deploying to Iraq as part of the British Army's commitment to Operation Telic in April 2004.

On 1 May Beharry's company was involved in a mission to resupply an isolated Coalition outpost in Al Amarah, with his platoon forming the company reserve. When a foot patrol became pinned down, Beharry and his platoon were sent in to extract them. En route they came under heavy and sustained attack by rocket propelled grenades (RPGs) that wounded the platoon commander, the vehicle's gunner and a number of soldiers in the rear of the Warrior. Beharry immediately moved the Warrior forward through the ambush position, but was hit again by RPGs, which caused the Warrior to catch fire and forced Beharry to open his driver's hatch. Despite this, he led the six vehicles of his platoon through the ambush, while under constant fire that destroyed his hatch, forcing him to drive the Warrior with his head exposed to enemy fire. When they finally reached the Coalition outpost, he extracted his wounded platoon commander and gunner and escorted the shocked and disorientated soldiers

▼ *Private Beharry's VC (left), presented to him by the Queen at Buckingham Palace on 27 April 2005.*

from the rear of the vehicle to safety, before
finally collapsing himself from sheer exhaustion.

Despite this he was on patrol again a month
later, on 11 June, serving as part of a quick
reaction force aiming to cut off an insurgent
mortar team in Al Amarah. As the unit was
moving towards the suspected mortar launch
point, with Beharry's vehicle in the lead, they
were ambushed and an RPG detonated on the
vehicle, only 6 inches (15cm) from Beharry's
head, causing severe injuries. Other rockets hit
the rest of the vehicle, injuring the commander
and other members of the crew. Despite his
condition, Beharry managed to keep control of
the Warrior. He reversed it out of the ambush
zone and continued until the vehicle crashed
into a wall, at which point he lost consciousness.

These two incidents were worthy of the
highest honour available to the British Army,
as his citation confirms: 'Beharry displayed
repeated extreme gallantry and unquestioned
valour, despite intense direct attacks, personal
injury and damage to his vehicle in the face of
relentless enemy action.'

> " *Beharry displayed repeated
> extreme gallantry and
> unquestioned valour, despite
> intense direct attacks,
> personal injury and damage
> to his vehicle in the face
> of relentless enemy action.* "

Soldiers from the Afghan National Army and 3rd Battalion (The Black Watch) The Royal Regiment of Scotland board an RAF Chinook in fading light en route to an operation in Helmand Province, Afghanistan.

PRIVATE MICHELLE NORRIS
MC

awarded 15 December 2006 • Iraq • RAMC

▼ Private Michelle Norris dodged enemy fire to reach her commander, who had been injured during fighting in the Maysaan Province in June 2006.

Michelle Norris was only 18 when she became the first woman ever to be awarded the Military Cross for her actions in Iraq in June 2006. Exposing herself to enemy fire, she climbed on top of the Warrior AFV (Armoured Fighting Vehicle) in which she was travelling to administer life-saving first aid to its wounded commander.

Michelle Norris had only recently finished basic training as a combat medical technician when she was deployed to Iraq in April 2006, where she acted as a company medic, travelling out with the troops on operations so that she could be on hand to provide vital immediate first aid in the case of anyone being injured.

Norris was attached to C Company, 1st Battalion The Princess of Wales's Royal Regiment, part of the Queen's Royal Hussar's Battlegroup, and on 10/11 June she was with the company as they went on a search operation in the town of Al Amarah in southern Iraq. This operation developed into a major firefight and the Warrior AFV in which Norris was travelling was diverted to help rescue a Warrior that had become bogged down. At this point the Warrior in which she was travelling came under heavy fire and the vehicle commander was severely wounded in the face. Unable to access the turret cage of the vehicle, Private Norris dismounted the Warrior and climbed on top of the vehicle to provide emergency first aid to the wounded commander. Throughout the whole

The crew of a Warrior AFV prepare their vehicle for a search operation in Iraq.

time she was doing this, she was under fire from the same sniper who had shot the commander of the Warrior. She remained there under fire until the gunner of the Warrior pulled her into the turret and she managed to get the vehicle commander into the back of the Warrior. There, she carried on treatment until they reached the evacuation site. Her citation makes clear the risks she took: 'Despite the very real risks from sniper fire, heavy small-arms fire and rocket-propelled grenade, she deliberately ignored the danger to her own life in order to administer live-saving first aid to the commander of the vehicle.'

When they reached the evacuation site the baton was taken up Major William Chesarek, a US Marine Corps officer on exchange with the Fleet Air Arm's 847 Naval Air Squadron. Major Chesarek was providing radio relay services for the troops on the ground when he realised that there was a serious casualty on the ground. Landing his Lynx helicopter, he loaded the wounded Warrior commander on board, even though he was forced to leave a crewmember on the ground to do so. For his actions, Major Chesarek was awarded the Distinguished Flying Cross, the first US serviceman to receive the award since the end of the Second World War.

> *Despite the very real risks from sniper fire, heavy small-arms fire and rocket-propelled grenade, she deliberately ignored the danger to her own life in order to administer live-saving first aid to the commander of the vehicle.*

▲ Marine Major William Chesarek displays the DFC he was awarded for his actions on the night of 10/11 June 2006.

MAJOR SIR TASKER WATKINS

VC, GBE, PC

awarded 31 October 1944 • Normandy • Welch Regiment

As a young lieutenant, Tasker Watkins, who died in 2007, was awarded the Victoria Cross for an assault on a German machine-gun post in the struggle for Normandy in August 1944. His courageous bayonet charge in the face of enemy fire silenced the position, and he fought off the enemy counter-attack that followed, allowing his men to withdraw to safety.

▼ *Tasker Watkins following the presentation of his VC by King George VI at Buckingham Palace on 8 March 1945.*

Tasker Watkins was born in Glamorgan and joined the Welch Regiment as a private soldier at the outbreak of the Second World War in 1939, being granted an emergency commission in May 1943. He was posted to a reinforcement group in Normandy in June 1944, before joining the 1/5th Welch Regiment in July. On the evening of 16 August 1944, the battalion was advancing near the village of Bafour as part of the Allied effort to close the Falaise Pocket and trap the German 5th and 7th Armies. While advancing across a cornfield, the 1/5th Welch came under sustained German machine-gun fire that caused heavy casualties and left Lieutenant Watkins as the only remaining officer. He immediately led his men forward in a charge, wiping out two German machine-gun posts. As he moved forward to clear an anti-tank gun position, his Sten gun jammed and he threw it into the face of a German soldier in front of him before shooting him with his pistol.

When the inevitable German counter-attack appeared, Watkins organised his 30 men to

> **His superb gallantry and total disregard for his own safety during an extremely difficult period were responsible for saving the lives of his men, and had a decisive influence on the course of the battle.**

conduct a firm defence in the face of around 50 attackers, before launching a bayonet charge to drive them back. With night falling and his position isolated and surrounded, Watkins decided to withdraw through the flank of the German forces. Coming across another German machine-gun position, he ordered his men to scatter and attacked it on his own with a Bren gun, silencing it and enabling his men to withdraw to safety. The citation for his VC emphasises his personal contribution to the successful withdrawal: 'His superb gallantry and total disregard for his own safety during an extremely difficult period were responsible for saving the lives of his men, and had a decisive influence on the course of the battle.'

After the end of the war, Watkins became a lawyer; he was knighted in 1971, made a privy councillor in 1980, and rose to be Deputy Chief Justice of England in 1988. He was also closely involved with the Welsh Rugby Union, and served as its president from 1993 to 2004.

▼ *British troops wend their way through the ruins of Lisieux, Normandy, 22 August 1944. The last days of August saw the culmination of the effort to trap the German 5th and 7th Armies in the Falaise Pocket, the battle that ended the Normandy campaign.*

MASTER AIRCREWMAN RICHARD TAYLOR
QGM

awarded 6 March 2009 • MV *Riverdance* rescue • RAF

Richard Taylor was the paramedic winchman on board the RAF search-and-rescue Sea King helicopter that was called out to rescue those aboard the ferry *Riverdance*, which had foundered in atrocious condition in the Irish Sea on the night of 31 January 2008.

▼ *From left to right: Air Force Cross recipient Flight Lieutenant Lee Turner, and The Queen's Gallantry Medal recipients, Petty Officer Aircrewman Kevin Regan and Master Aircrewman Richard Taylor, at Buckingham Palace after collecting their medals.*

The MV *Riverdance* had been struck by a heavy wave, causing her cargo to shift. She had lost all power and began listing at 60 degrees in heavy seas, some 10 miles (16km) off the coast near the town of Blackpool. The duty search-and-rescue Sea King at RAF Valley was scrambled to rescue those aboard the ferry, who were now in severe danger. The winds were at storm-force level and visibility was appalling.

Master Aircrewman Taylor was the man who was winched down to the rolling deck in order to rescue those stranded on board the stricken vessel. Although the conditions on board the ship were extremely difficult, with the vessel listing and pitching at all times, Taylor managed to winch eight of the passengers up to the Sea King before taking them to hospital in nearby Blackpool.

Having been relieved by a Royal Navy rescue helicopter, the RAF crew returned to the ferry at just after 0400 hours to finish off the rescue. This was made more difficult by the fact that the ferry was now stranded on a sandbank. The cargo had broken loose, and was moving freely around the deck, causing an additional hazard for the already tired winchman. Despite this, Taylor was winched once more to the deck and organised the

rescue of the remaining eight passengers, before finally winching himself up to the Sea King with the final pair – an exploit that tested the power of the winch to its very limits.

All of the crew of the Sea King were honoured for their role in this daring rescue, with the pilot, Flight Lieutenant Lee Turner, being awarded the Air Force Cross for his consummate skill in handling the aircraft in such dreadful conditions. Richard Taylor was awarded the Queen's Gallantry Medal, as was Petty Office Aircrewman Kevin Regan.

▲ *The stricken ferry MV* Riverdance *is battered by the high seas as it lies grounded off Blackpool.*

An RAF Sea King HAR3/3A. This particular aircraft is a search-and-rescue or SAR Sea King from 22 Squadron, based at RAF St Mawgan, Cornwall. The Westland Sea King HAR3 entered RAF service in 1978 and the 3A in 1996; both marks of aircraft are used in the Search and Rescue (SAR) role. The aircraft are operated from six locations around the UK, with each location supporting two aircraft. The SAR squadrons provide 24-hour cover around the UK throughout each year. Each squadron maintains a 15-minutes readiness state during daylight hours and a 45-minutes readiness state during the hours of darkness.

STAFF SERGEANT OLAF 'OZ' SCHMID

GC

awarded 19 March 2010 • Afghanistan • Royal Logistics Corps

Olaf 'Oz' Schmid, who was killed in action on 31 October 2009, was awarded the George Cross for four months of tireless work dealing with improvised explosive devices (IEDs) in the dangerous environment of southern Afghanistan. Time and again he succeeded in removing these devices in the most difficult of circumstance before his untimely death.

▼ *A bomb disposal expert from the Explosives Ordinance Disposal (EOD) approaches an IED.*

Born and raised in Cornwall, Olaf Schmid joined the Royal Logistic Corps in 1996 and trained as an ammunition and bomb disposal specialist. He excelled in this role in operations in Northern Ireland, Yugoslavia and Kosovo, and was promoted to staff sergeant in 2008. In June 2009 he was deployed to Afghanistan as a High Threat Improvised Explosive Device Disposal (IEDD) Operator in Helmand, attached to the 2nd Rifles Battlegroup, and was straight away thrown into action in Operation Panther's Claw – a major British-led effort to extend ISAF control over Helmand and drive the Taliban out of the region. While attached to the 2nd Rifles, Staff Sergeant Schmid cleared some 64 IEDs to allow the battlegroup to move around with a degree of confidence and safety. In doing this, he was hampered by the fact that the situation on the ground in Afghanistan made it very difficult to use much of the specialised gear developed for the task, such as heavy-duty protective equipment and remote-controlled vehicles.

In the course of these operations he succeeded in opening the Pharmacy Road in

◀ Staff Sergeant Oz Schmid on duty in Afghanistan. The conditions during the war in Afghanistan meant that it was impossible to wear the heavy-duty gear that offered a degree of protection when dealing with IEDs.

▼ Oz Schmid's widow, Christina, holds the GC conferred on her husband by the Queen following a private ceremony at Buckingham Palace on 2 June 2010.

> " His selfless gallantry, his devotion to duty, and his indefatigable courage displayed time and time again ... saved countless military and civilian lives. "

Wishtan Province on 9 August 2009, spending 11 hours clearing a large number of linked IEDs in temperatures of over 45°C (113°F). His actions allowed an isolated company to be supplied, and kept the operations of the battlegroup going. This was typical of his experience in the four months he served in Afghanistan.

On 31 October, after having dealt with three IEDs already, Schmid was on his way to the next job. A searcher discovered a command wire in the alleyway they were travelling down, and, tracking the wire to its source, Staff Sergeant Schmid found a complex IED linked to multiple charges. It was while he was attempting to defuse this that he was tragically killed. His citation (above right) speaks of Schmid's 'selfless gallantry and devotion to duty'.

LANCE CORPORAL ANDREW WARDLE
MC

awarded 24 September 2010 • Afghanistan • Yorkshire Regiment

▼ A soldier from the 1st Battalion The Royal Welsh is pictured briefing members of the ANA in preparation for an operation in Helmand Province on 27 January 2001. The British Army takes its mentoring role for the ANA very seriously.

Andrew Wardle was awarded the Military Cross for a wide range of actions in Afghanistan over his six-month tour with 2nd Battalion The Yorkshire Regiment from September 2009 to March 2010. From attacking the Taliban and locating improvised explosive devices (IEDs), through to rescuing a small child under fire, Corporal Wardle was heavily involved in action during his tour of operations.

Corporal Wardle was born and brought up in Hetton-le-Hole, Sunderland, and joined his local regiment, the Yorkshire Regiment. He was deployed with them to Afghanistan in September 2009 as part of Operation Herrick XI. Wardle's specific role was to be leader of an Operational Mentoring Liaison Team in Helmand Province, southern Afghanistan. Such teams are responsible for providing training and mentoring to the Afghan National Army (ANA), as well as serving in a liaison role to ensure that there is sufficient coordination between the ANA and other ISAF forces. These teams have an essential role in assisting the development of an independent, robust and resolute national army that can take up the role of defeating the Taliban insurgency.

It was certainly an eventful tour, as Corporal Wardle found in the space of a couple of days. First he was concussed when he was knocked to the ground by the blast of an rocket-propelled grenade (RPG) during an operation north of Musa Qala in Helmand. Then, a few days later he was involved in another firefight with the Taliban and witnessed a young child being shot and falling on the open ground, exposed to fire from both sides. With no thought for his own safety, and in full view of the Taliban positions opposite him, Wardle ran 50 metres (164 feet) across the open ground, picked up the child and returned to cover, where the young boy was given first aid and transferred to hospital by helicopter. These, and other incidents over the six-month tour, warranted the award of the MC, as is made clear from his citation (quoted top right).

▲ *Lance Corporal Andrew Wardle with the MC presented by the Prince of Wales at the investiture ceremony at Buckingham Palace on 9 December 2010.*

▶ *The Yorkshire Regiment use their Regimental Freedom rights to march through the City of York with their newly presented Colours on 19 June 2010. The regiment contains four battalions, three regular and one TA. Andrew Wardle served with the 2nd Battalion in Afghanistan.*

ROSEMARY POWELL

Royal British Legion poppy seller

Rosemary Powell, now aged 96, was present at the very first of the Royal British Legion's Poppy Appeals in 1921. Now, on the occasion of the Legion's 90th anniversary, she has been able to celebrate the continuing success of both the Royal British Legion and the Poppy Appeal.

▼ *Rosemary Powell aged 6.*

The year 1921 saw the launch of both the British Legion and the Poppy Appeal, which had its origins in a similar appeal launched in America in 1920. Having moved across the Atlantic, the idea was enthusiastically supported by the British Legion's first President, Earl Haig, who urged everyone to wear a poppy on 11 November in memory of the fallen of the First World War. Just after midnight on 11 November 1921, the first poppy was sold in London, and supplies rapidly ran short throughout the capital. One basket auctioned at Christie's for nearly £500. In total, around £106,000 was raised that year, a staggering success considering that the appeal had been promoted for only a few short weeks.

Rosemary Powell vividly remembers selling poppies on Twickenham Bridge as a 6-year-old in 1921. Her family were living in London while waiting for their house in Cumberland to be renovated, and, like most families of the day, they had a close connection with the events of the First World War. Rosemary's father had served in the Indian Army throughout the war, and been badly wounded at the battle of the Somme, before serving in Afghanistan with the Camel Corps. Also, living close to the Royal Star and Garter Home for disabled servicemen in

◄ *Rosemary Powell outside No. 10 Downing Street, prior to attending a reception given by the Prime Minister, David Cameron, to honour the Royal British Legion on the occasion of its 90th anniversary.*

Richmond, her family was keenly aware of the sacrifices made by the generation of servicemen that had fought in the First World War. So they were happy volunteers when the first Poppy Appeal was launched.

As was the case across London, the poppies in Richmond soon started to run out, and Rosemary was left on Twickenham Bridge while her mother rushed to a nearby newsagent to buy crepe paper to make more.

Rosemary's association with the military and the Legion has continued throughout her life: her husband served in the Royal Navy during the Second World War, being present at the Battle of North Cape, the last great battleship action that saw the sinking of the German capital ship the *Scharnhorst*; and when they lived in Pau in France for many years, they would also place a wreath, provided by the Royal British Legion, on Remembrance Day.

Now, in the year of the Legion's 90th anniversary, Rosemary provides a link with its very early days and its first fundraising efforts to support ex-servicemen and servicewomen. In 2010, those efforts raised £115.2 million, including a record £35 million for the Poppy Appeal.

ACKNOWLEDGEMENTS

I would like to thank the following for their invaluable contributions to the book, which I am hugely proud of. Without their hard work, support and enthusiasm this project would never have got off the ground and I am very grateful to them all: Marcus Cowper; Iain MacGregor, Kathy Dyke, Elen Jones, Martin Topping, Richard Augustus, Joanna MacGregor and everyone else at Collins; all the team at the Royal British Legion; General Sir David Richards; the staff at the picture archive of the Imperial War Museum; and, of course, my literary agent Humfrey Hunter.

Matt Croucher GC

PICTURE CREDITS

The publisher is grateful to the following for permission to use copyright images:

Australian War Memorial: pp4–5, 23 (bottom) E03183; p22 H15713; p85 (top) 059358; p87 (top) ART27515; p105 (top) 081389; p140 FAI/70/0595/VN; p141 (top) ART27773; p141 (bottom) LES/69/0589/VN. **Barry Turner Photography:** p199 (top). **Crown Copyright:** p7 Dave Husbands, Royal Navy; p9 CPI Dan Beardsley, RLC; p37 RAF Museum Collection PC73/4/529; p190 UK MOD 2011; p191 UK MOD 2011; p212 UK MOD 2011; p213 (both images) UK MOD 2011; p222 UK MOD 2011; p230 UK MOD 2011; p231 (bottom) UK MOD 2011; p233 (bottom) UK MOD 2011; p236 UK MOD 2011; p238 UK MOD 2011; p239 (top) UK MOD 2011; p243 (bottom) UK MOD 2011; p244 UK MOD 2011; p246 UK MOD 2011. **Dame Kelly Holmes:** p 215. **Getty Images:** endpapers, p6 Indigo/Getty Images, p23 (top), p45 (top), p71 (bottom), p149 Popperfoto/Getty Images, p167 (top), p181 (main), p193. **Heathcliff O'Malley** p219. **Imperial War Museum:** pp2, 241 B 9614; p13 A 18492; p17 (bottom) PST 10994; p18 HU 088589; p19 (top) VC 623; p19 (bottom) FIR 009220; p20 EPH 9356; p21 (top) Q 047894; p24 A22029, p25 FL 22540, p26 00247; p27 (top) Q 115096; p27 (bottom) FIR 008255; p28 CBM 1210; p29 (top) LD 700; p29 (bottom) SP3129; pp30-31 Q 31493; p32 EPH 7240; p33 SP3129; p34 UNI 012268; p35 Q 2879; p36 UNI 011617; p38 Q 67483; p40 C 1081; p43 (bottom) EPH 2313; p44 EQU 421; p45 (bottom) Q 67556; p46 UNI 0012559; p47 (top) A 22310; p47 (bottom) Q 68079; p48 TR 856; p49 C 5009; p51 (bottom) CH 14264; p52 ART 1322; p53 Q 18121; pp54–5 CH 1500; p56 VC 269; p57 (top) Q 37880; P57 (bottom) WEA 800; p58 E 18980; p59 ART LD 5915; p60 Q 12015; p61 (bottom) CH 1521; p62 HU 59359; p63 HU 57656; p65 (top) CH 1700; p65 (bottom) CH 2530; p66 E 014578; p70 ART LD 869; p72 MH 000020; p73 (top) A 5826; p73 (bottom) MH 004981; p75 (top) A 019636; p75 (bottom) ART LD 005441; p76 UNI 005484; p77 (top) H 40971; p77 (bottom) FIR 008008; p78 NA 19483; p79 (top) HU 2125; p79 (bottom) E 29095; pp80-81 SE 002138; p83 (top) HU 98917; p83 (bottom) EA 33757; p84 HU 004569; p85 (bottom) ART LD 005618; p86 C4109; p87 (bottom) ATP10774B; p88 OWIL 65659; p89 (top) HU 68042; p89 (bottom) FIR 11372; p90 KOR 649; p91 (top) KOR/U 11; p91 (bottom) OMD 1634; p92 GOV 2739; p96 MH 31495; p97 KOR 000616; p99 HU 3161; p100 FL 8441; p101 (top left) A 32737; p101 (top right) FL 7265; p102 OMD 4263; p103 MH 31478; p104 EPH 003357; p105 (bottom) BF 011040; pp106–7 A 033601; p108 CH 158; p109 CH 9250; p110 GOV 10661; p111 GOV 12027; p112 SP967; p113 Q 21299; p114 BU 5302; p117 (top) HTF-2006-043-427; p118 FES 65 156 120; p123 (top) FKD 359; p123 (bottom) FKD 3144; p124 FKD 2100; p125 (top) FKD 541; p125 (bottom) SFPU-N-1084B-25; p126 ART LD 3823; p127 (bottom) PST 14524; p128 GOV 13418; p129 A 034778; p131 R 28937; pp132–3 TR 18614; p134 GOV 9361; p135 GOV 9111; p136 C 465; p137 (top) C 457; p137 (bottom) CH 15213; p138 ART 2626; p139 Q 114867; p142 A 10137; p143 (top) A 21819 p144 MH 30556; p148 HU 043396; p150 MH 30626; p152 TR 1799; p153 NA 21427; p154 MH 15239; p155 (top) ART LD 7424; p155 (bottom) A 28783; p156 HU 56936; p158-9 MH 30550; p163 Q 9271; p164 ART 16420; p165 GLF 54; p166 HU 98866; p170 FKD 002028; p174 BOS 215; p176 FKD 314; p178 OMD 2718-2733; p179 HU 56125; p180 MUN 3867; p181 (inset) Newgass 001; p182 FKD 2601; p183 BU 3154; pp 184–5; p186 ART LD 3926; p187 HU 2242; p188 HU 50160; p189 ART LD 3055; p194 MH 2240; p195 (bottom) BF 11094; p196 GLF 1425; p201 NA 15298; p202 OMD, 3700-3709; p203 CI 842; p204 B 7510; p205 E 006751; p207 (top) ART LD 2720; p207 (bottom) HU 20288; p208 MUN 4843; p209 (bottom) BOS 21; p210–11 GLF 000762; p220 UKLC-2000-049-006-019; p221 (bottom) UKLC-2000-049-001-016; p229 (top) A 029378; p229 (bottom) A 018930; p233 (top) HQ MND (SE) 03 053 234; p240 HU 2304. **Kevin Capon:** p216. **National Portrait Gallery, London:** p61 (top), p127 (top). **Pat Hyde:** p218. **Pete Winner:** p168, p169. **Press Association:** p8 PA Archive/Press Association Images, p10 PA Archive/Press Association Images, p11 PA Archive/Press Association Images, p68 PA Archive/Press Association Images, p69 (top left) PA Archive/Press Association Images, p71 PA Archive/Press Association Images (top), p95 (top) AP/Press Association Images, p115 Ron Bell/AP/ Press Association Images, p117 (bottom), p130 Kirsty Wigglesworth/Press Association Images, p157, p160 Carl Court/Press Association Images, p162, p167 (bottom), p173 (top), p173 (bottom), p175, p191 (top) Anthony Devlin/Press Association Images, p192, p195 (top) AP/Press Association Images, p198 Fiona Hanson/Press Association Images, p199 (bottom) Toby Melville/Press Association Images, p200 AP/Press Association Images, p206 AP/Press Association Images, p217, p221 (top) Adam Butler/AP/Press Association Images, p226, p227 AP/Press Association Images, p228 Sean Dempsey/Press Association Images, p231 (top), p232, p234 UK Press/Press Association Images, p235, p242 Lewis Whyld/Press Association Images, p243 (top) John Giles/Press Association Images, p247 (top) Anthony Devlin/Press Association Images, p247(bottom) Anna Gowthorpe/Press Association Images. **RAF Museum:** pp 39, 50, 64 Iain Duncan, p98 Charles Brown Collection. **Royal British Legion:** title page, chapter openers, pp14–15, 16, 17 (top), p42, p43 (top), p69 (top right), p94, p95 (bottom), p120, p121 (top), p121 (bottom), p146, p147 (top), p147 (bottom), p172, p214, p224, p225 (top), p225 (bottom), p248, 249. **Times/NI Syndication:** p51 (top), p116 Ben Gurr/The Times/ NI Syndication, p122 Jon Enoch/The Times/NI Syndication, p161 Arthur Edwards/The Sun/NI Syndication, p245 (top) Lee Thompson/The Sun/NI Syndication. **US Library of Congress:** p21 (top) LC-USZ62-8054. **US Marine Corps:** p239 (bottom). **US Navy:** p143. **Wayne Mills** p209 (top) wiki.

While every effort has been made to trace the owners of copyright material reproduced herein and secure permissions, the publishers would like to apologise for any omissions and will be pleased to incorporate missing acknowledgements in any future edition of this book.

INDEX

Entries in *italics* indicate photographs.